D0392478

SHOOT TO THRILL

SHOOT TO THRILL
The History of Hockey's Shootout

MARK ROSENMAN AND HOWIE KARPIN

Foreword by
"Jiggs" McDonald

SPORTS
PUBLISHING

CONTENTS

DEDICATION

This book is dedicated in loving memory of my father
Morris Rosenman, and my sister Suzie. If they were both
still alive today they would have bought enough copies
themselves to make this book a #1 best seller. I'm also
dedicating this book to my wife Beth, son Josh, daughter
Liana, mother Estelle, sister Cheryl, as well as all my
extended family and friends whose love and support
inspire me to follow my passions and dreams.

FOREWORD

A PROLONGED SLAPPING of the stick on the ice to honor Mark and Howie for having the ingenuity to unravel the mysteries of hockey's shootout. This gimmick was added to the best team sport of them all in the early '90s and has done nothing but at times confuse fans, players, coaches, officials, and broadcasters as well as bring people out of their seats for a regular season game.

To this day, I vividly recall of sitting alongside Bill Clement as we broadcast the hockey games at the 1992 Olympic Winter Games from Albertville, France, for TNT when all of a sudden the game was tied after overtime and we were faced with the first ever shootout. It was one of the rare times that I wasn't fully prepared or up to speed on what was about to happen. They do what again? We both kind of shrugged our shoulders as the players huddled, officials gathered at the timekeeper's bench. Seemingly everyone was unsure of what was about to happen. *This is no way to decide an outcome*, I thought to myself. First one side, then the other, back and forth.

Sure, I knew Eric Lindros had scored, but was it really the decisive goal?

There have been so many innovations added to the game for one reason or another.

Being in hockey all these years has given me an opportunity to make special relationships along the way, so despite being adverse to the shootout rule myself, the National Hockey League arguably presents the greatest players in the world and they are the ones participating.

Hockey is such a beautiful game that even though the shootout reduces a team sport to one of more individuality, the skill and movements that make up an attempt are still to be marveled and admired.

Within the confines of this book, you have many of hockey's greatest minds and voices offering an array of opinions on the shootout rule.

Additionally, the anecdotes and trivial notes dispersed throughout this book will enlighten any hockey fan and will give you a perspective into how and why this rule was added from those who were and are still directly involved.

You're about to enjoy the rest of the story as you read on.

Well done, Mark and Howie!

—"Jiggs" McDonald

PREFACE

SINCE IT WAS founded in 1917, the National Hockey League has established time-honored traditions and provided many memorable moments. But in the world of professional sports, there is always a need for change and growth.

A labor dispute wiped out the entire 2004-2005 NHL season. When the league resumed play the following year, a salary cap was implemented along with a new rule where ties would no longer be part of the everyday standings and a "shootout" would decide the winner.

Change brings resistance and the shootout rule has created a controversy that has inspired healthy debate within the hockey fraternity.

The "penalty shot" has always been one of the sport's most dynamic and exciting plays, so the thinking among hockey officials was "why not decide a game with a series of penalty shots [a.k.a. shootouts]?" The shootout would be similar to the method of deciding tie games that had been in use in soccer since the 1980s.

The NHL needed change. Ten years ago, hockey was attempting to enhance a passionate, but relatively small, fan base, while competing with the likes of Major League Baseball, the National Football League, and the National Basketball Association for paying customers.

From players, officials and broadcasters, to the passionate fans who live and die with the sport, everyone has an opinion on the "shootout rule." In *Shoot to Thrill*, we've chronicled numerous opinions and interspersed them with informative and humorous anecdotes that have made the sport of hockey and the National Hockey League unique in its own way.

We hope that passionate and casual hockey fans will enjoy this book as much as we did in putting it together.

1

The History of the Penalty Shot

THE REFEREE'S WHISTLE stops play because a penalty is called, but this is not just any penalty. The ref points towards center ice, which means the "most exciting play in hockey" is about to take place as a penalty shot is called.

The puck sits dormant on the center ice dot, waiting to be carried by the player who will go one-on-one with the goaltender with a clear chance to score a goal.

A penalty shot is awarded when a player who is clearly ahead of the defense on a breakaway is fouled and loses the scoring chance. This can result after a number of other infractions (see "Rule 24" later in this chapter).

A penalty shot is awarded in lieu of a minor penalty, so the team that's fouled does not also receive a power play from a single infraction.

The penalty shot is reported to have originated in the Pacific Coast Hockey Association. League President Frank Patrick was tired of seeing deliberate fouls on players who had good scoring chances so he introduced the concept of a "free shot."

On December 6, 1921, the first penalty shot goal was scored by Victoria Cougars' forward Tom Dunderdale—who was a two-time PCHA scoring champ and the only Australian-born member of the Hockey Hall of Fame—against Hall of Fame goaltender Hugh Lehman of the Vancouver Millionaires.

(In 1926, the forty-one-year-old Lehman became the first ever goaltender of the Chicago Black Hawks. In the 1927-28 season, Lehman played only four games and was appointed head coach but was fired at season's end.) Dunderdale took the shot from one of three dots painted on the ice, approximately 35 feet

Frank Patrick introduced the concept of a
"free shot."
(Stuart Thompson via Wikimedia Commons)

from the goal. At that time, players had to skate to the dot and shoot the puck from the dot.

The National Hockey League added the penalty shot rule for the 1934-35 season.

In the first season of the new rule, the puck was placed in a ten-foot circle, 38 feet from the goal mouth. The shooter could take the shot while being stationary within the circle, or shoot while moving, as long as the shot was taken within the circle. The goalie had to be stationary until the puck was shot, and no more than a foot in front of the goal mouth. The current NHL rule book states the following:

> *24.1 Penalty Shot – A penalty shot is designed to restore a scoring opportunity which was lost as a result of a foul being committed by the offending team, based on the parameters set out in these rules.*

A penalty shot is called when these infractions occur:

(i) Deliberate illegal substitution
Rule 68

(ii) Intentionally dislodging the net from its moorings during the course of a breakaway
Rule 63

(iii) Intentionally dislodging the net from its moorings when the penalty cannot be served in its entirety within regulation time
Rule 63

(iv) Falling on the puck in the goal crease
Rule 63

(v) Picking up the puck with the hand in the goal crease
Rule 63

(vi) Player on a breakaway who is interfered with by an object thrown or shot by a defending team player
Rule 53, Rule 56

(vii) Player on a breakaway who is interfered with by a player who has illegally entered the game
Rule 70

(viii) Player or goalkeeper throws or shoots an object at the puck in his defending zone
Rule 53

(ix) Player on a breakaway who is fouled from behind
Rule 24

Hall of Fame goalie George Hainsworth made the first save of a penalty shot in NHL history.
(Wikimedia Commons)

On November 10, 1934, the National Hockey League's first penalty shot was awarded to Montreal Canadiens forward Armand Mondou. He was stopped by Hall of Famer and former Toronto Maple Leafs goaltender George Hainsworth.

Three days later, St. Louis Eagles forward Ralph "Scotty" Bowman beat Montreal Maroons goaltender Alec Connell to record the first penalty shot goal in NHL history.

Carolina Hurricanes left wing Erik Cole made history when he was the first player to be awarded two penalty shots in the same game. In November 2005, the Hurricanes were in Buffalo when Cole had two chances to beat Sabres goaltender Martin Biron. Cole scored on one of the penalty shots but Biron denied him on the other attempt. "I made the move I wanted, but not the shot I wanted," Cole said about his missed penalty shot.

Erik Cole was the first player in history to be awarded two penalty shots in the same game.
(Dan4th Nicholas via Wikimedia Commons)

In his next game, Cole became the second player in NHL history (LA Kings center Esa Pirnes was the first in 2003) to be awarded penalty shots in consecutive games, but couldn't beat Florida goaltender Roberto Luongo.

There have been two instances where an NHL team has scored on two penalty shots in one game.

On February 11, 1982, Canucks centers Thomas Gradin and Ivan Hlinka scored penalty shot goals against Detroit Red Wings goaltender Gilles Gilbert.

Because he was one of the players on the ice when the infraction occurred, Hlinka took the penalty shot because of an injury. Detroit defenseman Willie Huber took down Canucks right wing Stan Smyl from behind. Smyl was injured and had to leave the game. Kerry Fraser worked that game in Detroit as a twenty-eight-year-old NHL referee. "Hlinka scores on the penalty shot,

Joe Thornton scored one of two penalty shot goals for the same team in the same game for the second time in NHL history.
(Wikimedia Commons)

everything gets thrown out of the stands that wasn't nailed down at me. Reed Larson took a water bottle and launched a forty-yard pass towards me. I moved my head and it slipped by me and I gave him a misconduct, fought my way out of the building almost, there was police with me but there was a fan that I just about came to blows with," Fraser said.

The second time occurred when the San Jose Sharks hosted the Washington Capitals in December 2009.

Left wing Ryane Clowe and center Joe Thornton each scored on a penalty shot against Capitals goalie Michal Neuvirth.

Clowe was tripped by Capitals defenseman Mike Green to set up his opportunity while Washington defenseman John

Ryane Clowe joined Thornton as the other
penalty shot goal scorer.
(Ivan Makarov, via Wikimedia Commons)

Montreal winger Max Pacioretty was the first player to be awarded two penalty shots in the same period.
(Lisa Gansky (Flickr), via Wikimedia Commons)

Erskine was ruled to have thrown his stick in an attempt to stop Thornton on a breakaway.

In February 2014, Montreal Canadiens winger Max Pacioretty became the first player to be awarded two penalty shots in the same period, but he failed on both attempts versus Vancouver Canucks goalie Roberto Luongo.

There was a historic incident, involving a penalty shot, which mirrored baseball's famous "pine tar" incident in 1983. (Because Yankees' manager Billy Martin argued that the Kansas City Royals' George Brett had pine tar too far up the barrel of his bat, Brett had a home run taken off the board, after the fact.)

Kerry Fraser was working a game late in the 1986-87 season between the Kings and Calgary Flames in Los Angeles, when a penalty shot goal was disallowed.

Flames winger and Hall of Famer Joe Mullen had been awarded a penalty shot with 35 seconds left in the third period after Kings goalie Al Jensen threw his stick.

"Joey Mullen was a couple of goals shy of his 50th goal and think he got stuck on 47 that year," said Fraser. "It's a one goal game in Los Angeles, there had been a penalty shot I awarded towards the end of the game to Joe Mullen."

Kings HC Mike Murphy told center Bernie Nicholls to lobby Fraser by invoking "Rule 20(e)" of the National Hockey League Rule Book.

Fraser said the Kings "asked to measure Joey Mullen's stick" and he responded as follows: "OK, here's the process if you want to do that, you have to wait 'till he takes the shot." (At the time, Rule 20(e) stated that there would be a measurement, but only after the shooter had taken his shot and only if he scored. The rule has since been changed.) Fraser said, "If he scores the goal and his stick is measured and found to be illegal, then I take the goal away, if however the goal isn't scored and the stick is legal, you're going to get a bench penalty."

Nicholls said, "Let me think about it." Fraser replied, "Well, you better think pretty quickly because we're going to go here and you have to make the decision now and not after the goal or failed attempt." After Nicholls and the Kings decided to take the measurement, Fraser described what happened next.

"Joey Mullen goes down and scored the goal. He is wildly excited, he's in the corner, he's banging the glass, raising his arms. I skated over and I said, 'Joey, I need your stick please,' and his face turned white like the blood drained from his face. 'I got to measure your stick, they made an appeal.'

"Mullen said, 'Kerry, come on, I'm going for 50 goals, I got a $50,000 bonus.'" Fraser told Mullen, "Well, I hope your stick's legal," and went to measure the stick.

Fraser said, "It was illegal, clearly illegal, but based on the fact that he told me he was moving towards the $50,000 goal, I measured it a couple of times. I had help from the linesmen to make sure the gauge was at a fixed point of the heel, that it didn't slip, measured it two or three times and each time I measured it, it was clearly illegal, so I took the stick."

The measurement showed that the curvature of the stick was off by 1/8 of an inch, so the goal was disallowed.

Fraser was frank with the future Hall of Famer. "Joey, you got a goal taken away." I told him, "the way you score you'll score your fifty. You got a couple of games left, don't worry," Fraser said. (Unfortunately for Mullen, he finished with 47 goals that season.)

From the 1921-22 season through the 1966-67 Stanley Cup Playoffs, there were 8 penalty shots called in postseason without a goal being scored. Since that time, there have been 62 penalty shots that have resulted in 21 goals being scored. Hall of Famer and former Toronto St Patrick's right wing Babe Dye, who once scored 5 goals against the Boston Bruins in 1924, was awarded the first postseason penalty shot but Vancouver's Hugh Lehman stopped it.

The first penalty shot goal in the playoffs was scored by Minnesota North Stars center Wayne Connelly when he beat Hall of Fame goalie Terry Sawchuk of the LA Kings in 1968.

"I don't recall too much about the play the penalty was called on," said Connelly. "I thought I was going to have a breakaway and going in all alone, I forget the player that interfered with me and I didn't get my shot off and when the referee (John Ashley) blew the whistle I never ever thought about a penalty shot."

Up to that point, no one had ever scored a penalty shot goal in a Stanley Cup Playoff game, something Connelly was not aware of when he set up to take the shot.

"It didn't mean too much never realizing at the time that no one in the playoffs had scored a penalty shot goal and knowing it was against Terry Sawchuk which was the premier goalie of my time at that time and when I took the shot it went in," Connelly said.

The North Stars center had an idea of what he wanted to do against the future Hall of Fame goaltender.

Connelly said, "I was told by one of my teammates, Ray Cullen, that he knows Terry Sawchuk a little bit and he is going to wait and let me make the mistake, so he's going to more or less stand there and hope that I make the mistake by either losing the puck or hitting him with it or missing the net and actually when I went down I took a look and I could see the left side open and I just shot it and it went right in off the goal post."

When asked about the media reaction to the first penalty shot recorded in NHL Stanley Cup play Connelly said, "It didn't seem like a big deal at all. Let's go back to 1968 with the coverage. We were at home in Minnesota when I scored it and there wasn't much, you only had a couple of press around so it wasn't a big deal at the time. It wasn't 'til years later that I even found out that that was the first one scored. Over my career that's one record that no one can take."

There wasn't a penalty shot goal scored in the Finals until the first game on June 5th, 2006, when Edmonton Oilers defenseman Chris Pronger "lit the lamp" by putting one past Carolina Hurricanes goaltender Cam Ward.

Referee Mick McGeough called a penalty shot after Hurricanes defenseman Niclas Wallin covered the puck in the

Chris Pronger is credited with scoring the first penalty shot goal
in Stanley Cup Finals history.
(Chris Pronger (Flickr), via Wikimedia Commons)

crease with his hand. Oilers Coach Craig MacTavish had to
choose a player who was on the ice at the time to take the shot.

Pronger had not participated in any of Edmonton's
16 shootouts during the season (the shootout rule made its debut
for the 2005-06 regular season), which made MacTavish's selec-
tion of him surprising to many. Pronger took the shot and beat
Ward on the short side to end a streak of eight previous misses
in the Finals.

Carolina won 5-4 and would go on to win the Stanley Cup
in seven games. After the game, Ward said, "Pronger came in a
little bit slower than expected, he made a really good shot. That's
a tough area to stop."

In the 1985 Stanley Cup Finals, there were two penalty shots
that were stopped in two straight games by Edmonton Oilers
goalie Grant Fuhr.

In game four, Fuhr denied Philadelphia Flyers center Ron
Sutter as the Oilers took a 3-1 lead in the series with a 5-3 win.

Two days later, Edmonton clinched their second straight Stanley Cup championship in an 8-3 blowout. With the game in hand, Fuhr stopped Philadelphia's Dave Poulin on the fourth penalty shot ever called in a Finals game.

In the 1994 Stanley Cup Finals, a penalty shot became what many consider to be a turning point.

The New York Rangers were trying to end a fifty-four-year drought without winning a Stanley Cup while the Vancouver Canucks were seeking their first.

The Rangers held a 2-1 lead in the series but the Canucks had a 2-1 lead in the second period of game four when New York defenseman Brian Leetch took down Vancouver winger Pavel Bure, who was on a breakaway.

"It was a good call," Leetch said, after referee Terry Gregson had pointed towards center ice, signaling a penalty shot.

Bure had scored 60 goals during the regular season. Rangers' goaltender Mike Richter would be one-on-one with one of the best players in hockey on the sport's biggest stage.

Bure took the puck at center ice and tried to put a forehand shot past Richter on the right side, but the Rangers goalie stuck out his leg and got his right toe on the puck to deny the speedy winger who was nicknamed "the Russian Rocket." "He came out from the net and that's why I couldn't shoot," said Bure.

"I have seen Bure use that move before," said Richter, "I wasn't looking for that particular move, though. He's too good to think he has only one move."

The save sparked the Rangers, who tied the game late in the second period and then went on to win the game and the series in seven games.

"It was a classic confrontation between one of the most, if not the most, electrifying forwards in the game right now and an outstanding goaltender who hasn't been given much recognition throughout the playoffs," Rangers Coach Mike Keenan said at the time. "That was the biggest stop he's ever made in his career, I'm sure."

One for the Record Books

Martin Biron was the Philadelphia Flyers' goaltender when he faced a penalty shot in game one of the 2008 Eastern Conference Semi-Finals vs. Montreal.

At the 6:32 mark of the second period, a penalty shot was called and Montreal's Andrei Kostitsyn had a chance to cut into the Flyers' 2-0 lead, but Biron made the stop to temporarily preserve the lead.

Montreal went on to down the Flyers in overtime, but Biron entered the record books as one of the goaltenders to deny a penalty shot in a Stanley Cup playoff game.

Biron didn't feel there was much of a difference facing a penalty shot in a playoff game as opposed to a regular season game.

"As a goalie, the playoffs factor, unless it was an overtime game seven, you kind of just put it aside," Biron said, "the penalty shot is important enough, the game's important enough, you don't have to worry about it."

Six-time Vezina, two-time Hart Trophy winner and future Hall of Fame goaltender Dominik Hasek faced five playoff penalty shots—four with Buffalo and one with Detroit—and allowed just one goal to Toronto's Mats Sundin in 1999.

✳✳✳✳✳

Even though they feature the same basic premise, a shootout and a penalty shot have their differences.

While a shootout provides the excitement of deciding a regular season game, the event becomes almost premeditated when the game gets to overtime, but the penalty shot is spontaneous and with more of a sense of urgency. Only one team and one shooter get the chance to score a goal (that does count on the scoresheet) against a goaltender, that only needs to make one stop instead of three.

Going into the 2014-2015 season, shootouts are not part of the Stanley Cup Playoffs, but penalty shots can take place in a postseason.

2

Fit to Be Tied

WHETHER IT'S POSITIVE or negative, everyone has an opinion about the shootout. And that includes those who've played, coached, or worked in hockey in one capacity or another.

We spoke with past and current players, coaches, executives, journalists, and broadcasters who are close to the sport to sample their opinions on the shootout rule.

NY RANGERS RADIO AND NHL ON NBC PLAY-BY-PLAY ANNOUNCER KENNY ALBERT

"I am probably a little bit of a traditionalist in that I would rather have a winner and a loser. I didn't mind ties because a team could play hard and battle for sixty, sixty-five minutes and under the current system, if it goes to a shootout, it sometimes feels like a loss as it was a tie prior to that, but you look around the arenas during shootouts and the fans are on their feet and it's so exciting. I do agree that they should never go to the shootout in the playoffs, which, of course, they haven't done. I know the NHL has taken some polls and it's been overwhelmingly in favor of shootouts in the 70-80 percent range. So I don't mind it that much in the regular season because it certainly does add to the entertainment value, but in the playoffs I do like that they play until somebody wins the game. I think the shootout has led to some pretty memorable moments: you think back to the Marek Malík shootout at Madison Square Garden against the Washington Capitals. And I know they have outlawed the 'spin-o-ramas' this season, but Kaspars Daugavins couple of years ago against Tuukka Rask and Boston, so I think when we look back on some of the highlights from the last decade or so, shootouts are certainly going to be among the top plays we have seen in the regular season in recent years."

WASHINGTON CAPITALS CENTER NICKLAS BACKSTROM

"I like the shootouts. I think it's good for the crowd. It's never fun to end the game in a tie, so I'm good with the shootout. I think the shootout is more entertaining at the end of the games for the crowd and it's fun for us to pick three shooters and they can be heroes for the game, and I think that's good."

NY ISLANDERS CENTER JOSH BAILEY

"I prefer the shootout. It's a spectator sport and I think the fans really like it. I remember when it was first introduced and whenever there was a game that went to the shootout you were pretty excited to see it and I think from the fans' perspective, and even the players', it's pretty nice to end with a winner and a loser."

FORMER NHL GOALTENDER MARTIN BIRON

"I bounce back and forth all the time; I don't really know if there is a system that is perfect. Going home with a tie is kind of anticlimactic like you just, 2-2 game, both teams played good and at the end you almost just shake hands at center ice and say 'Hey, good job, you want to go for a drink after the game?' That's like kind of what it was, but I find that there was a rewarding process if you got a win, that you got 2 points and the other team didn't get any; now you get a win and the other team is still feeling good about themselves because, alright, so we just lost in the shootout, no big deal, loss doesn't really count. Teams are saying they are 10-12 games over .500, but are they really 10-12 games over .500? They lost eight shootout games, they're only four games over .500, really, when you go wins-losses, so there's a misconception and they can be swayed either way. I don't know if there really is a perfect setup, but play until somebody wins and maybe we will have some late nights in the middle of December and that might be fun."

BOSTON BRUINS CENTER PATRICE BERGERON

"I think I like the current system just because there's a winner even though it doesn't really dictate the game but there's still at least a winner at the end of the game. I think it's good. Not everyone likes it, but I think for the fans it's definitely something that makes it exciting for the end of games. But [it's] definitely better if you win the game instead of just losing in the shootout, [which] is always disappointing."

NHL Commissioner Gary Bettman

"I like the shootout in the way we use it. I wouldn't like the shootout in the playoffs, and the fact is I like the shootout better than ending a game in a tie. And so the issue is: can we tweak overtime so maybe there are slightly fewer shootouts? But the fact is, no matter what your opinion is—from the media or hockey person or fan—watch the buildings when the shootouts are going on. Everybody is on their feet. Everybody is interested. Everybody is watching. When games were ending in ties, that wasn't so much the case in overtime.... Nobody is looking for a fundamental adjustment. We're looking more for a tweak to see if maybe we can get a few more games decided in overtime, but the shootout is a concept that's here to stay."

Former NHL center Henry Boucha

"I am old school, no shootout. Win the game in regulation or split the points.

"I have to admit from the league's side though it's not a bad idea, most people like it and it is exciting for the fans. It keeps the fans in the building longer and they buy food and beverages."

Former NHL goaltender Brian Boucher

"Personally, I like the old system better, from a players' standpoint. Because I feel like what's happening now is that specialists are brought in for that particular situation and I don't necessarily know that that is hockey at that point. Come playoff time it's sudden death and you play as long as need be, so I guess in a way that makes up for it, but the shootout is not hockey, it's a skills event and certainly some guys are better at it than others, both shooters and goaltenders. But I guess for the sake of having a result maybe it's a good way to do it with maybe a certain amount of time to get it done. I remember the one year the Rangers and Capitals went fifteen rounds [on November 26, 2005, with the Rangers winning], but typically that doesn't happen. It's usually over in five rounds, so you can get people in and get people out. I understand it but I prefer the tie or maybe even going into a ten-minute overtime and maybe go 3-on-3 or something to that effect, at least that's still hockey at that point."

NY RANGERS DEFENSEMAN DAN BOYLE

"I've been through both systems. I think old-school people would probably want to eliminate the shootouts and I would consider myself one of those. But it is about pleasing the fans and I think somehow the majority of the fans want the shootout, so we have to listen to what they want. So I am open to both, but the ties were more old school, I guess. I think now you see certain teams late in the game and possibly in overtime maybe being a little more conservative defensively, trying to get the game to the shootout because they feel strong with their goaltending or that their shooters are going to win the shootout. So I would much rather see it done in a 5-5 or even a 4-4 situation."

NEW YORK POST HOCKEY COLUMNIST LARRY BROOKS

"I understand the desire to have every game end with a winner, I do. It's not 1960 anymore, it's not 1970 anymore. I just wish there was a better vehicle than a one-on-one competition. I have a hard time accepting that as legitimate, but I don't think either alternative is optimum. Again, I don't think you want to see ties because you know the stakes in the game are so high now there's just so much money involved and the difference between making the playoffs and not making the playoffs is millions of dollars, and so you know that in a tie game with ten minutes to go, teams would just shut down and play for the point and the final ten minutes of a game would be unwatchable. So I do get the desire to eliminate ties, but the shootout to me dilutes the competition that preceded it and if there was another way to do it, it'd probably be preferable."

FORMER CALGARY FLAMES GENERAL MANAGER CRAIG BUTTON

"I wasn't big on shootout when [it was] announced. First time I saw and could feel the excitement of the fans, I switched 180 degrees. I love it. If you don't like the shootout to decide games then make sure as a team, you decide them in regulation or overtime! The impact, in my opinion, is that coaches play it tighter through regulation to ensure a point and then take their chances in overtime or [the] shootout. [This] is because parity means each and every point is so important."

NEW YORK ISLANDERS CENTER CASEY CIZIKAS

"I like the shootout because it brings excitement. I think everyone wants to see it. I hate the game ending in a tie so you always have to have a winner and I think the shootout is a perfect way to settle it during the regular season. It's tough when you don't win in regulation, but the shootout becomes so important because you never know when it comes down to the end of the season and you miss the playoffs by one or two points and that's [because of] a shootout loss you had. So the shootout has a huge impact on the NHL."

Former NHL Defenseman and Hockey Analyst Bill Clement

"I don't like ties. I like to have a winner, so in that respect I am in favor of the shootout, but only as a mechanism to decide ties. I think it has kind of run its course in the NHL only because the novelty of it has worn off. Also, it was an attraction coming out of the lockout when the NHL did such a fabulous job of sort of reinventing itself. I think the novelty wore off to the point where I am in favor of having the game decided in overtime now. So while I am a proponent of no games ending in ties, I think the deciding mechanism for concluding a winner should be something other than a shootout."

San Jose Sharks Center Logan Couture

"I started out in the OHL where we had the shootout, so I enjoy it. I think it adds excitement to games. As a fan I love watching games go into shootouts. It's a little different as a player, though. It always makes me nervous."

Logan Couture is a fan of the shootout.
(Derek Ortiz (Own work - SJ Sharks Teal And White Game), via Wikimedia Commons)

DETROIT RED WINGS SENIOR VICE-PRESIDENT JIM DEVELLANO

"I like the previous system, and as a matter of fact the Detroit Red Wings voted to keep things the way they were and we had voted against the shootout. In some cases because of the shootout, teams have missed the playoffs. Some have made the playoffs because of it. I just think it's a silly way to decide the outcome of an important event."

NBC PLAY-BY-PLAY ANNOUNCER MIKE "DOC" EMRICK

"Being a resident dinosaur I reluctantly have to go along with what the league decided and the fans liked it, so if they like it, I shouldn't be so presumptuous as to throw my own preferences ahead of theirs, so I'm with the shootout. I think TJ Oshie may have done more to sell me on the shootout than anybody did, (see "Shot Heard 'Round the World"). I remember seeing him and I said, 'I remember before you

The #1 TV Voice of the NHL doing his thing.
(Lisa Gansky, via Wikimedia Commons)

took the fourth of your shots, you looked over at the referee for the signal and you had a smile on your face.' He said, 'Well it was pretty funny' and I'm thinking I didn't think it was! But he said, 'Well it was getting pretty funny' so I suppose now I have a different feeling about it than I did at first. I know that there are some people that grudgingly refer to it as an exhibition and I used to watch teams come into Philadelphia and play for ties, because at least they got a point out of it. Now at least there's more entertaining, so compared to what I saw thirty-five years ago or so, before we even had a five minute overtime, I'd say yeah it's better."

BUFFALO SABRES GOALTENDER JHONAS ENROTH

"I prefer the shootout. I think you need a winner every game, and it's a little more exciting for the fans and the players, so I think it's a little more fun. It puts a little more pressure on the shootout takers and the goalies, and at the end of the season those shootout points are pretty important."

BOSTON BRUINS LEFT WING LOUI ERIKSSON

"I think it's fun for the fans maybe, to see some shootouts, but I think it's more if you play overtime and try to score. It's more intense and it's more fun for us [the players].

"It's good for the fans. They want to see them and yeah that's my thought."

1980 GOLD MEDAL WINNING TEAM USA CAPTAIN MIKE ERUZIONE

"I like the Shootout. It is exciting, the fans like it. I can't believe they eliminated the 'spin-o-rama' this season, because I thought the object of the shootout was to be entertaining but during the regular season I like the shootout. Hockey's a long season and if you're playing games that have overtime after overtime, it would be crazy and too much of a grind. From a fans' standpoint, the shootout has been exciting. I think they like to go away knowing that there was an outcome, so my opinion overall is that the shootout has been good for the game."

HALL OF FAME CENTER PHIL ESPOSITO

"I do not like the shootout, but I am truly from the old school. A lot of people like it. C'est la vie."

HOCKEY HISTORIAN STAN FISCHLER

"What's not to like? There isn't a game where the fans aren't standing on their feet during a shootout watching it. Of course if you lose you're sad but that's not the point, the point is it's a plus, what the heck is wrong with that? The impact of the rule over ten years is that there are a lot of people who are upset about it because they are hockey purists living in another era, but times change. I remember when I started covering hockey there was no such thing as a cell phone, now I have a phone that doesn't have a cord and I still can't believe it. Time marches on, there is absolutely nothing wrong with something new as long as it's valid and this is valid. Breakaways always have been something exciting and now this is a new type of breakaway and it's very decisive at the end, it's super melodrama."

FORMER NHL LEFT WING NICK FOTIU

"I love the shootout, I think it keeps the people in the building. Years ago you would have to wait for a penalty shot, but it's great now to see the interest for the shootouts, it's great. Look in the stands now, look at how many people stay in their seats now with 30 seconds left in a tie game. Years ago when the people felt the game would end in a tie they would leave to beat the traffic, now the interest is still there to the very end. Back in the day we worked at breakaways to end the practice to see who would have to deliver the drinks to the whole team; it was a lot of fun."

SIRIUS XM HOST ANGELO "ZIG" FRACASSI

"I don't care for the shootout. As a fan and, later, media member, I didn't mind ties, especially in a game where both teams deserved a point after a well-played game. I totally understood the NHL needing to get fans back after the work stoppage of 2004-05. Sometimes, it drags and drags, almost taking away the value of the 65-minute game. I thought it would have been phased out by now, but, unfortunately, it appears here to stay.

"I might be off the wall on this idea, but, if the NHL's so intent on an 'extra point,' give each team a conditional power play. Say the Bruins are playing the Canadiens. Boston was chosen to get a two-minute power play. They score and Montreal gets a chance. However, if the Canadiens scored while killing the penalty, the game ends right then and there. If Boston scored, then Montreal scored on theirs, then the game ends in a tie."

FORMER NHL REFEREE KERRY FRASER

"The shootout is really exciting. It's a penalty shot, it's a skill competition. What I don't like about it is that it becomes an all-star game competition. The rule has been fabricated and slid to the point of tolerance where a player can do almost anything and it gives [an] unfair advantage over the goalkeeper. You can almost stop, you can spin around, you can do a lacrosse stick move and throw it, anything that is deemed to be an athletic type play is allowed. The rule was never intended to be that way. From the start of a penalty shot rule in the book when I arrived in the 70s, so, as players have become more skilled, more skilled hands and doing the kind of things that bring fans out of their seats at all-star competition contests, they've allowed that to be part of the game. In a regulation game points in shoot wins are really important for a team either making the playoffs or not making the playoffs and I just think it's totally [an] unfair advantage that the players have over the goalkeepers with what they are allowed to do, which is now pretty much anything. I think there needs to be a conclusion to a game. I know that there were times where we went into a five-minute overtime and it was the road team just hoping to secure a tie and it became boring, there was no all out go for it. I think that the shootout has provided that they get the point when we go into overtime and there's a shootout advantage of an extra point so I like the concept. I just don't like the fact that they allow anything to happen that previously the referee would blow his whistle and stop the play on a penalty shot if a player did a lot of the things that we see taking place now."

FORMER NHL LEFT WING ADAM GRAVES

"I certainly like the shootout as a fan, because I am a big fan but I am also a traditionalist, so I would not want to see it in the playoffs. I like the idea of going to overtime, because

I am also a soccer fan and watch the World Cup. I always thought it was a tough way to lose a game. For me with the National Hockey League and the shootout, I think it's fantastic. In all thirty cities, when the shooter for the home team gets ready to take that first step, everyone in the stands are standing because it's a crescendo of excitement and I think it's fantastic. It's exciting there are so many talented players and the skill level, the speed and the goaltending has never been better at the National Hockey League level. I think that is certainly on display and you get to see that whether you're watching TSN, ESPN, or all the different websites that follow hockey. The shootout makes the highlights every night because it is so exciting and skill based."

FORMER NY RANGERS DEFENSEMAN RON GRESCHNER

"I don't see anything wrong with the overtime part of it, the shootout part, I think, is somethin' that's not. I watched soccer this year, some of the World Cup soccer and I don't think it's pretty fair that they play a ninety-minute game and a thirty-minute overtime, then you play a team in the shootout and you end it scoring a goal. I think if they're going to do the overtime thing and it ends up nobody wins at that particular moment, then it stays at one point each. If you win in overtime, you get two points, the other guy gets nothing. You shouldn't get a point for having overtime and losing. If you lose the game, you lose the game. I disagree with all that. You get two points for winning and you get a point for losing. I know some of the fans love the shootout, I think it really is entertaining but I don't like the way it is, I wish they would go do something else. Maybe, three on three or four on four."

On the impact that the shootout rule has made on the NHL:

"To be honest with you, I hardly ever stick around to watch the shootouts. I watch sometimes, if I'm at the Garden, but if I'm at home, I don't sit there and go like 'Oh man I can't wait for the shootout to come now.' I like hockey, I don't like things that are tricky. I don't like the games ending like that. If you're gonna do an overtime, do an overtime with the team getting three points for winning and the other team gets one. You know what happens right now, especially now, because you watch the games and the teams are so well put together. The coaching is so great, the players are really great, they're all in good shape, they're fast, so a lot of times the last eight, ten minutes of a game are like watching paint dry. I like to see the entertainment of it, either you win the game or lose the game, you don't get a point for hanging around. It could be the last period of a game, the last ten minutes of a game, it's the most boring part of a game that I've ever seen in my life."

On teams playing for the point in the waning minutes of a game:

"I think that's unjust to the fans, if there was a case that you couldn't get that one point by playing to the end, teams would play a lot differently. That's robbing the fans. Years ago, when we got a 1-1 game, we would play to the end too. It was 1-1, it ended up 1-1, so you got the point, but, if you're gonna have that, have a team that ends up in a tie in a regular time frame of a game, don't give them any points, winning team gets two."

NY METS PITCHER MATT HARVEY

"I like the fact that there is a winner and a loser. When you play that long and hard, you should have a winner and a loser. The shootout atmosphere is really exciting. It just adds another level of excitement."

FORMER NHL DEFENSEMAN (AND YES, ONE OF THE "HANSON BROTHERS" IN THE MOVIE *SLAP SHOT*) DAVE HANSON

"Strictly as a form of entertainment, of the two choices, I prefer the shootout. Simply due to the excitement it provides, the one-on-one challenge of a shooter with creative moves or a laser wrist shot going up against a goalie who is battling for his teammates and self-reward is an added source of pure entertainment that no other major sport has. It doesn't necessarily allow the better team to get the win and get their deserved points, and it rewards the weaker team with points that they wouldn't necessarily have gotten through team play."

Co-author gets a "Slap Shot" from the Hanson Brothers.
(Courtesy Mark Rosenman)

FORMER NHL GOALTENDER GLEN HEALY

"I am not a big fan of the shootout. It results in certain teams not making the playoffs. The Rangers are a good example. They didn't make the playoffs on an Olli Jokinen shootout, Philadelphia did and they went to the Stanley Cup finals. That being said, fans typically don't leave, so I guess it's good for the fans, it's good for the game, it's good for the players, so it doesn't matter what I think because I'm not playing anymore. I just think you could add on another couple of minutes and you could finish games in a traditional way."

FORMER NHL RIGHT WING ANDERS HEDBERG

"I don't mind the shootout, it's not the perfect ending, but it is a better ending than a tie. I think that the specific skill of scoring on a breakaway has been exposed much more than it ever was, which means that players have to really excel in that particular area and they do and it's a fabulous exhibition where lots of difficult things are being done on the ice. Sometimes it's also an exhibition of not very good things because there are misses and not very good ones."

MONTREAL GAZETTE HOCKEY COLUMNIST PAT HICKEY

"As a fan I like the shootout, as a purist I hate it. I like the way it was before and if they thought they had to settle something you come up with something better than the shootout, but it certainly is exciting. I think the fans love it. I like watching it but, as a purist, someone who has been watching and covering for fifty years, it's not my way of doing things."

Hall of Fame defenseman Mark Howe

"Most hockey people they prefer having the ties and not the shootouts. Last year, our team, we played four, maybe five, really good games in a row and then you go into the overtime, and then you go to the shootout and you lose and you feel like you lost, even though you get the one point. If it ended the other way, say it's a 1-1 game, you go away feeling good because you played a good hockey game, and you earned a point. The other thing I don't like about the shootout is it really inflates the standings. You look at a team in the past that had a one hundred point season, now you can have 100 points by having a ninety point season and winning ten shootouts, I think it inflates the numbers. The bottom line is what keeps the people in the seats. I think generally the average fan tends to like it, but I think I'd prefer not to be that way."

NHL Network and MSG Network analyst E. J. Hradek

"I don't like ties so I was happy they have a way of bringing the game to a conclusion, a win or loss in the regular season. I mean obviously we are only talking about the regular season here, you can't play all night logistically so you can't have an overtime that goes on forever. The NHL Players Association would never agree to have that to begin with, so it's a solution. I think the people who come to the building pay so much money now for tickets, it's kind of a different era and you talk to the fans in the building, they seem to like it. Those of us who watch the game or cover it and have been around it a long time, obviously it's not the perfect solution to deciding a hockey game but I think when you pay over $100 or $200 for a ticket and you come in and the game ends in a tie, for me that's something from another time, so I just like they have a solution. I think fans kind of like it, it's obviously not a perfect answer to the problem, but I don't have a big problem with it. Yeah, there are times I see a great game and it's disappointing it ends in a shootout, but as a regular season game goes, I don't mind it. The thing I really would love to see more than anything is forget about the overtime points and just have a win is a win and a loss is a loss. Accept it for what it is and if you win a shootout you get two points and if you lose you get nothing. I think it would be easier when you are selling to fans because some people say well you want to 3-2-1-0 system which makes sense but it's more confusing and it's just more columns. I would love to just see wins and losses. For me, in a perfect world, let's have the shootout. You win it, you get the two points, if you lose you don't get anything."

Former NHL goaltender Corey Hirsch

"I hate games that end in ties to be honest. You pay all this money and then the game ends in a tie and you're like really? I do think they can do things in overtime that make the chances of a shootout even less than they are now. The shootout is good but it's a contest and yet we all watch it. The shootout also has made the standings a lot tighter as teams are getting points just for the tie where you're automatically guaranteed a point, so a lot of teams towards the end of the game are just playing for that tie. It also makes it pretty advantageous to have a good shootout player and goalie on your team; there's twenty-nine other teams in the league that would love to have T. J. Oshie on their team right now, that's for sure."

NHL Network Analyst Billy Jaffe

"I have always been a fan of just good hockey and if that means a tie happens, then a tie happens. I'm old enough to be called older but not Grandpa so I'm ok with the tie. I get the value of a shootout because we are in an entertainment business and it seems like a lot of people, fans, really enjoy it. Because of that if it helps grow the game I'm ok with it but I don't personally love it. It's a tough way to decide a team sport in what is essentially a skills competition, I would not consider myself an ultra traditionalist. There's a lot of things about the game that I'd like to see changed. I just have a hard time with certain things with the shootout. The fact that now they went to regulation and overtime wins only has made me much more ok with the shootout because it doesn't factor into certain playoff positions."

Former NHL Goaltender Brent Johnson

"I prefer the first way it was done. I like sticking to the roots. I am just one of those type of traditional guys, the game was there and obviously they changed it to increase revenues and to get people to watch more often, but I liked it ending in a tie, I really did. I think it's a weird way to get a 'W' to me because only a few number of team members actually get in the shootout to try and get a win for the team, which to me takes away the whole team sport concept. That being said, I enjoyed playing in them. I had a good record in the shootout. It was something that was fun but I still prefer the tie. I think for the league it's been great. You get positive public feedback, everyone thinks it's an exciting part of the game, but truthfully, a traditionalist like me, it's not a game like, guys can go in at their leisure and do whatever kind of moves that they want to. Even though they have reeled that back a little with taking the spin-o-rama out this year, I think that the fan feedback has been great. When it comes down to it, to get people to watch and go and pay money to see these exceptional games and if it ends in a tie and then goes into a shootout, if the fans like it then, so be it. What one retired goalie thinks doesn't matter, it's what the consumer likes."

FORMER NHL CENTER KEVIN KAMINSKI

"I prefer the shootout definitely. I think it's exciting. It's one on one, you got your best goalie in and your three best shooters. I think it's exciting for the fans. You're going to get a point anyway and to have an opportunity to win it in a shootout, I think is great. From what I have seen, either at the games or on TV, when it goes to the shootout it seems the fans sure enjoy it. I don't know what the current players think of it but I think it's absolutely fabulous to tell you the truth."

FORMER NHL AND STANLEY CUP–WINNING HEAD COACH MIKE KEENAN

"I don't like it and the reason I don't like it is because it has influenced the standings and the final playoff positioning in the league and I think it's an individual skill, it's not a team skill. Even if they went to three-on-three or four-on-four for a longer period of time in the overtime, that would be more palatable for me. The shootout is an individual skill and it's put the teams out of the playoffs. They had more opportunity to be in a playoff position but lost it because of a shootout."

Sirius XM NHL Radio host Mick Kern

"Initially, I was in favor of 'kissing my sister.' It's what I grew up with, and change for change sake is rarely a productive thing. Once the shootout was implemented, and we were treated to the likes of Marek Malik performing his magic in front of a previously scornful crowd, I was sold on the marketing possibilities the shootout provided. In a sound bite world, the shootout delivered, on a silver platter, jaw dropping hockey highlights to an often reluctant US sports media to salivate over. In addition, don't judge the success of the shootout by polling anyone born before 1990. Ask the kids. Almost universal approval; and there are your future consumers. I have become a believer, though a ten minute over time would also be nice."

Former NHL left wing Derek King

"I don't mind either way, but I think giving more points for a win would be a system to think about. It might make teams play for the win in regulation time. The shootout has been great for the fans. I say if you score the winner in a shootout it goes towards your stats, though."

Boston Bruins center David Krejci

"I personally would prefer a tie because I think it's more fair than the shootout. At the end of the season it could be a big difference. Look at Jersey last year, so I'd prefer ties."

Former NHL left wing Nick Kypreos

"I'm a bit of a traditionalist. I don't really particularly like games decided on a skills competition and at the end of the day it's exactly that, but I think that coming out of the lockout in 2004 that was something that the fans were looking forward to. I think they've embraced it and you know I'm older now and the game's not tailored for me anymore. It's the younger generation, the younger kids and I think they just love it. They think it's exciting, not too many people leave when there's a shootout and I think it's here to stay."

WASHINGTON CAPITALS CENTER BROOKS LAICH

"I like the current system of the shootout, ties just ended kind of boring, as players you were 'ah' it was a tie. At least with the shootout there's some emotion. Sometimes it's good, sometimes it's bad, but at least the fans have a result when they leave the building. I think the shootout has really magnified the stars. I think the star players really get some exposure. Before, our sport was very much a blue collar team sport whereas other sports like basketball and football are star sports and I think the shootout has helped make our sport more marketable because fans really attach themselves to stars. I think it has helped our sport grow."

ESPN NY HOST AND NY RANGERS PLAY-BY-PLAY ANNOUNCER DON LAGRECA

"You know when it first started I was really excited about the shootout. I thought it was something new and different although I never had a problem with ties, but now I think it's gotten old. I'm tired of it, it's just a glorified skills competition, it doesn't tell you really who the better team is and I have no problem with ties. I think teams work too hard to get that extra point and then to give another point to a team just because they happen to be a little bit more skilled just doesn't seem right to me, so I wish we'd go back to the old way."

ESPN.COM HOCKEY COLUMNIST PIERRE LEBRUN

"I'm ok with the shootout existing only if we add an extra point to a sixty-minute regular victory, that's the imbalance. What I don't like in the system right now, is that it rewards mediocrity. I'll never forget when the shootout came into effect because it was actually before the lockout. People forget it was in Henderson, Nevada. I was one of five media members at the GM Meetings and no one had warned us of all these changes and I'll never forget sitting down and it just looked like a boring GM meeting. Colin Campbell of the NHL came out and has a notepad with things written on it and he says 'we are looking at taking out the red line,' the shootout and names about eight things and all our jaws drop, and eventually those would be a lot of the items that would transform the game after the 2004-05 lockout. I understand the fans love it. I just think if the shootout stays in the game there has to be more of a gap between winning a real game in sixty minutes and getting points for it, then getting a loser point in a shootout."

SIRIUS XM HOST BILL LEKAS

"I've never been a fan of the shootout. That may come from the fact that I grew up playing soccer, and didn't appreciate having to decide tie games with penalty kicks. It's always been an artificial ending to me, because the shootout doesn't incorporate all the facets of the game that come into play during five-on-five or even four-on-four hockey."

COLUMBUS BLUE JACKETS CENTER MARK LETESTU

"I don't mind either system, my preference would be that they don't give a loser's point. It takes away some of the aggressiveness in regulation especially towards the very end. Teams are just looking for the one point and then kind of throw caution to the wind in overtime, but I would prefer just two points for the win and nothing for the loser, but either way it doesn't bother me the way they decide the games. The shootout is exciting for the fans, and I don't know the numbers if attendance is up or down because of it, but it obviously has had an impact in the standings. You look at the New Jersey Devils missing the playoffs last season because they went 0-13 in the shootout. If they just get a few of those points they would have passed us, so it has a big impact on the standings. I think the overall excitement, the highlights you see at night on the sports shows has brought more notoriety to the game."

ESPN SPORTSCENTER ANCHOR AND NHL ANALYST STEVE LEVY

"I like the shootout. I know I am in the minority with all the hardcore real hockey people, but I like the shootout because it's fun and you know what, no one ever leaves, and the kids love it. I have seen kids disappointed when someone scores in overtime because they want to stay for the shootout and the hardcore hockey people, I understand, but we are in the entertainment business and we need to keep the kids in the building and keep people hanging around and whatever does that I'm in favor of. Now if they can figure out a way, make it end in overtime I'm good with that too, but the shootout is the perfect answer, it's just small enough. If there were a fewer of them

I'd be ok with that, but I surely prefer this system over the old tie system."

FORMER NHL DEFENSEMAN CRAIG LUDWIG

"It's ironic we are talking about the shootout, as I am watching the World Cup now and it's in the shootout. I think that for me personally being on the side that I am now, when you're sitting there watching games and talking about games, it's exciting for the fans, or let's put it this way, it was exciting for the fans, I think it's losing a little bit today. I think it was great. I used to tell everybody you know in today's game there are two times for me that everyone in the building stands up, regardless if you're the home fan or a visiting fan and you're in someone else's building as a fan. It's two times. It's the shootout and it's a fight, and that's kind of when I see everybody on their feet. For me personally being old school, I'm not crazy about the games ending in shootouts especially when they don't translate into the playoffs. I've been a fan of playing the game until it's over and understand it's about time and TV and everything else, so that kind of drives it but what's the most important part of a hockey game? It's the sixty minutes, so if you put more of an emphasis on the sixty minutes by doing something like three points for a win, two points for an overtime win and one point for a shootout or something like that so that the most important time to push at the end of a game is at the end of regulation. I guess I'm on the fence. I understand from a fans' standpoint, but I guess I'm more old school. I'm not a fan of giving a point away to someone that loses, that's my biggest thing. You lose a hockey game I don't know why you're getting a point."

NY Rangers goaltender Henrik Lundqvist

"I like that you have a winner in the end. You play hard for two and a half hours, you want to leave the rink as a winner or in some cases you lose, but it's still more exciting than to leave with a tie game, so I like the shootout."

Former NHL goaltender Clint Malarchuk

"I like games ending with a winner. The shootout gives us that. A tie game is just that . . . a tie. No winner, no loser. Games need a decision.

I think the overall impact has been positive. Fans love it especially state side. Personally, I'd like to see a modified overtime, three on three would be exciting with lots of scoring chances."

Former NHL defenseman and NY Rangers TV and Radio analyst Dave Maloney

"I never had a problem with a nicely played 1-1 tie game. I think that had an excitement to it on its own and actually given now how competitive the league is, I think there is a lot of good hockey being played that ties might not be a bad thing. As far as the shootout, if you could guarantee that every home team wins the shootout, because to me there is no bigger buzz kill to a game than a home team losing a shootout. I think the shootout is a bit of a gimmick, a specialized event and I probably don't have as much respect for it as I wouldn't have been one of the guys to shoot in a shootout back in my day. I may have been like a Marek Malík, 12th on the list, but I think it certainly created a buzz early for a league that was looking for something to create buzzes in different ways, but now we're almost ten years into this and I'm just not sure the buzz is still there. I think it gets down to a specialty event, one that really doesn't count as a tiebreaker, so there are a lot of things about it that I'm not sure are congruent to the game and yet it certainly seems like it's going to be around for awhile."

FORMER NHL LEFT WING STEPHANE MATTEAU

"I love the shootout, it's great for the fans, great to see the best players show their talent. It's not a perfect match for everyone, New Jersey probably would have made the playoff if there wasn't a shootout, but other teams made the playoff because of it."

FORMER NHL GENERAL MANAGER AND HEAD COACH DOUG MacLEAN

"The year I coached and went to the Stanley Cup Finals, I think we had 22 ties (10) that got us into the playoffs, but we would have had those points anyway but you know what, I kind of like it, the fans love it. When you are in management and you have a shootout at home and you lose, you hate it because all your fans leave ticked off, they don't care if you got a point, but they leave like you lost the game. That's the only thing I found frustrating about the shootout, is from a management perspective, the hometown fan, especially in certain markets don't get it, they don't get that that point is real important. They see it as a loss and they leave ticked off, other than that, I find it exciting. I enjoy the skill of it, I don't have a problem with it. I was in the meetings when we put it in and we had a ton of debate, lots of good hockey people were against it but I think it has worked pretty well."

WINNIPEG JETS HEAD COACH PAUL MAURICE

"From a coach's point of view, I like the game ending in a tie because I think you're left with a natural and true emotion of how the game played. You can lose a shootout game and you'll always feel terrible. There's a loss involved. And when you win one, then you probably feel better than you should have. From a fan's point of view, I love the shootout. That happened to me. I used to hate it, and then during the lockout one year I would drive three hours to Norfolk, one-way, to watch an American League game once a week. By the time I got there to watch the game, I wanted to see some excitement. I don't want to drive three hours for a tie, you know? I'm sure that's the way the fans feel. They paid their hard-earned money, they want to finish with some excitement. I love the shootout from their point of view; I'd like it to disappear from a coach's point of view. I think, to be honest with you, that we should take care of the fans first."

HALL OF FAME BROADCASTER "JIGGS" MCDONALD

"I would prefer the pre-lockout system, a tie is a tie. I don't think the point system the way we have the shootout set up is fair and I don't like the aspect of it being a skills competition that not everybody gets to participate. From the fans standpoint it's entertaining but from the purist standpoint, no, I do not like it. I don't think we need a definitive winner, I think a hard fought game with a team that's battling to get into the playoffs comes out of it with a point, the other team comes out of it with a point not two points. I'm all for an even strength overtime and then a five minute four on four, could even go three on three and if after those overtimes you still have a tie, so be it."

NHL on NBC analyst and former head coach Pierre McGuire

"I still think there's a spot for a tie in hockey especially when there's a good game. It's not so much about goals, it's about scoring chances and sometimes I think goalies should be saluted for the work they did for sixty-five minutes and if they can maintain a tie that's great. Now the shootout is for the fans and the fans clearly appreciate it. I've been in very few buildings when a shootout is going on when the fans aren't standing so I think that's a positive for the fans as well. I think the biggest thing is, somehow someway, I'd like to see the game decided with players playing rather than just the shootout. Kenny Holland in Detroit, the general manager there, has had some pretty creative ideas and we'll see going forward, but the shootouts worked some magic here since '05 when the new rules came in."

NHL Network analyst Bob McKenzie

"I don't mind the shootout, and part of the reason I guess I don't mind it is because I knew that it was coming. It wasn't going away and that it was sort of a peace offering to the fans. I think that Gary Bettman and the National Hockey League decided that this is something they felt they needed to do from a marketing point of view and as sort of a peace offering to the fans, so I don't mind it. I like the idea of settling games and there being a winner and there being a loser. Maybe they should get rid of the loser point to make it even more important but then that sort of goes back to trivializing it by putting the entire weight of the hockey game on a skills competition."

Sirius XM NHL Radio reporter Terry Mercury

"I prefer the pre-lockout system of ties because at least teams are playing and using their skill to decide the contest. I know a lot of people say yeah but there were too many ties and I agree with that, but the shootout, I'm sorry a one-on-one skills contest should not decide the fate of some teams' playoff hopes. You got to play the game to decide who gets to the playoffs, the overtime stuff, it just doesn't work. I would go four-on-four for the first five minutes of overtime, three-on-three for the next five minutes and I guarantee you 95 percent of the contests would be decided. Right now you got teams that don't belong in the playoffs because all they're doing is that they know that they've got that one point going into the shootout, so they don't even try to decide it in overtime. They go into a shell just to hold off the other team just long enough to pick up that point. They say fine, let's get into the shootout, but no I don't like that, because you know what you have to play to win. Every other sport plays to win except the NHL; sorry but you have to play to win."

Mark Messier: "It's about what the fans want to see."
(Brendan Lee (Flickr), via Wikimedia Commons)

Hall of Fame center Mark Messier

"We are in the entertainment business and if that's a way to settle a tie score for the entertainment for the fans, the fans will be the ultimate ones to decide if the shootout stays or goes. I'm not making decisions so it's not about me and what I think. It's about what the fans want to see and then the fans will dictate what happens."

NY Rangers TV analyst Joe Micheletti

"What the shootout has done for the league I think is given the fans a sense of excitement that wasn't there when you compare it to the old system of ties. In the old system when you could get a tie, everyone played for the tie, and so there was no opening it up, and so people sat there, the teams got the tie and everyone moved on. The shootout did an awful lot to inject some energy into finding a way to get a team an extra point; however, I think there are too many of them, and I think the league is trying to address that, and that's just what happens as new features evolve. What ends up coming to the forefront are the negatives and positives regarding it, so I think that is the belief around hockey that we see too many shootouts, and I am glad they are starting to make a few adjustments to try and lower the number of shootouts that we do see."

Former NHL defenseman and general manager Mike Milbury

"I enjoy a tie. I could handle it, but it seems like most of the fans wanted a resolution, wanted a final score or wanted to see a winner and the shootout accomplishes that, and the question now is for me should they carry that into a playoff situation? Not too many long, long playoff games this year but some of these real long ones just get slower and slower as time goes by, and I think it would really hold an audience if you had a shootout after one twenty-minute overtime period except in elimination games."

FLORIDA PANTHERS LIVE HOST CRAIG MINERVINI

"I covered the Panthers who were one of the worst shootout teams ever. The years I did the pregame shows I believe they ranked the lowest in the NHL, but I find the shootout exciting because I like the moves and the excitement of it; however, I am not one of those who ever had a problem with a tie. I thought in hockey a point, sometimes it was a good point, one where you battled back and got the point. I didn't mind them going to the five minutes to try and decide it and you still get a point. I didn't mind the tie."

NY RANGERS CENTER DOMINIC MOORE

"I like the shootout. I think it's something different for the fans to see during the regular season. It's a different aspect of the game that they don't get to see that often and they seem to get excited for it. The purists obviously don't like to see the games end like that. Sometimes but for the sake of the entertainment value I think there is something to be said for it."

FORMER NHL DEFENSEMAN JAYSON MORE

"It's good that the NHL tried the shootout system for entertainment reasons but I like the old way of ending games better. Initially it was new and somewhat exciting, however, too many teams go into games just playing for the tie. The unintended consequences are that some teams have the road mentality to keep it close, just play a boring game of dump 'n' chase hoping to steal a point at the end of the night and it affects the standings in a big way. It's also become somewhat of a goaltender competition as the scoring success rate is only 32 percent. Now the league has banned certain moves that can be used in the shootout so less advantage to the skilled players and that 32 percent. scoring rate will be reduced further."

FORMER NHL DEFENSEMAN AND 1980 OLYMPIC GOLD MEDAL WINNER KEN MORROW

"I like the shootout. I have been scouting for over twenty years so I saw it coming first through the minor leagues and then make its way to the NHL, but I look at the fans and that's what it is for me. When you see 17 or 18,000 people standing through the whole shootout, it's something we can give back to the fans. It's an exciting finish to a hockey game and it is a result rather than a tie. I don't know if the rule has helped or hurt teams. You look at the Devils last year. They had a tough time in the shootout, but I think the team had bigger issues than that if you are relying on shootout points to get you into the playoffs; so, in that regard I don't think the shootout has had a negative impact on the game."

NY RANGERS LEFT WING RICK NASH

"I like the shootouts for the fans' sake. I think it's hard on the players to have the whole game rest on their shoulders, but I think it's exciting for the fans and it's good to end the game with a winner and a loser."

FORMER NHL CENTER BERNIE NICHOLLS

"I prefer the shootout. I don't think any game should end in a tie. I just think the excitement the shootout has brought to the fans, the entertainment is amazing. You look at the highlights and see goals scored in the shootout by guys like Patrick Kane and others, I look forward to it every night. I know when I played, if they had it back then, I would have been one of the guys to take the shot and I would have loved it. The entertainment the shootout brings to the fans is amazing, so that and the fact that I don't like ties is the reason I like the shootout."

NY ISLANDERS CENTER FRANS NIELSEN

"I like the shootout. I think it is good for the fans but I don't think you should get as many points when you win in a shootout as if you win in regulation, so they should probably do it the European way. Three points for a regulation win, two points for an overtime or shootout win, so it means a little bit more to win in regulation, but I don't think they should take the shootouts away because I think it's good for the fans."

BUFFALO SABRES GOALTENDER MICHAL NEUVIRTH

"I prefer the shootout. I think it's a little more exciting for the fans and for the league. It's a gamble sometimes but I think we're playing for the fans and they enjoy it, and that's why we are sticking to it."

FORMER NHL CENTER AND NHL ON NBC ANALYST ED OLCZYK

"I know why we have the shootout. I don't mind the shootout format, but I'm a believer that if you win you get the full allotment of points and if you lose you get nothing, so if the shootout would be winner take all then I could live with it. I don't like that both teams get a point in a shootout."

HALL OF FAME DEFENSEMAN BRAD PARK

"I think the question (of what does he prefer, a shootout or ties?) comes down to what the fans want. Bonus points for one, bonus points for the other, but it's really what the fans want. I mean the hockey purist doesn't like the shootout. The hockey fan, we love to see the shootout. I just think there's a better way to do it. The only problem we have about shootouts now is that they don't want to let the results of the game be determined by the shootout, that's the hockey purist. I think they should have a shootout before the start of the third period every game, so the fans get to see a shootout. That means that one team has lost the shootout, they can't afford to play it safe going down the third period and into the overtime but they have a chance to win it. If they're tied and going into the overtime, they've already lost the shootout, they know they still have a chance to win the game but they've got five minutes to do it. If the game ends up in a tie after the overtime, that team (that wins the shootout) wins, which gives the losing team a chance to change the results."

NEW JERSEY DEVILS HOST DEB PLACEY

"I much prefer overtime and then a shootout. And although I love Ken Holland's suggestion of three-on-three and then a shootout, I think they have it right this year. Cleaning the ice and going back to the long change is the way overtime should be played, and we will see fewer shootouts. Why? Because there's no real reason to end in a tie when you can spend a few extra minutes to reward skill, both from the shooters and goaltenders, and determine a winner. The impact? It has cost a handful of teams a playoff spot, but the rules are the same for everyone."

NY ISLANDERS TV PLAY-BY-PLAY ANNOUNCER HOWIE ROSE

"I strongly prefer ties because they had value. Hockey is the only sport, at least eliminating soccer, apart from the World Cup, that cares. Hockey's a sport that computes its standings based on points, so a tie had value and I just felt that, yeah I mean it could be unsatisfying just as easily as you could feel like you stole something if you were down three goals going into the third period and came back and got a tie. It felt like you won and conversely if you blew a two- or a three-goal lead late in the game and settle for a tie, that point didn't taste very good, but I just abhor everything about the shootout. Frankly it's an insult to my intelligence. It's like 't-ball,' like everyone has to go away with something, baloney! The thing I hate most about the shootout, and it's a long list, is the one that I couldn't have predicted before they went to the shootout and that is it's supposed to be climactic, it's supposed to produce, never mind a winner or a loser, it's just supposed to be the apex of excitement in the game. I find it to be exactly the opposite. I find it to be a buzzkill, a complete letdown because by the time you get to a shootout presumably you have had a pretty spirited overtime. The four on four overtimes are great. It creates offense, and shoot, those overtimes you're at the edge of your seat, then when the five minutes are off the clock and the buzzer goes, it's like 'oh crap' can't we just go home now? This is a complete travesty, a shootout, you're going to decide a team game based on that."

On the impact that the rule has made on the NHL:

"It's created more interest. The guys that are shooting are generally the higher, well-known players, obviously because of their skills, so, it just brings another level of excitement for the fan. Obviously, it's probably not easy for a goaltender to be in that situation, but I think it's good. I wouldn't want to see a playoff game end that way, I think, you know the way system is in place for the season, it's okay, you know, the four on four creates some scoring chances, it's exciting."

Would he like to see any changes made?

"I haven't given that much thought. I guess, you look at some teams, you kinda play for a tie because you know you're gonna get a 'for sure' point. At the end of regulation, to let a team want it more at the end of regulation."

NY RANGERS TV PLAY-BY-PLAY ANNOUNCER SAM ROSEN

"I prefer the shootout because it puts closure on the game and I think fans have gotten to the point, and certainly I consider myself a fan where ties were not enjoyable, you didn't come out feeling good about it. Maybe you did if your team scored late in the game and came out with a point and had a tie but still I think we as sports fans want to see a winner and a loser. The traditionalists were accommodated that you still come out of the game with a point that you would have gotten for the tie and yet there was a winner. Now, the fact that it didn't end with actual play on the ice, that it was a skills competition if you will, doesn't bother me. You're still putting players out there competing against the goaltender and the goaltender is a key man. We have seen it on the world stage, in the Olympics, and World Cup Soccer. It's all part of the competition and I think if you accept that, you can accept the fact that a game is decided in a shootout. It's still the best players are out there, and your top goaltender is out there, and you were given a five-minute overtime period to try and decide the game; so I have been a proponent of it. I think the fans love it and I have enjoyed it."

BOSTON BRUINS GOALTENDER TUUKKA RASK

"I would like to just play the overtime and get rid of the shootout, personally. The fans like it so we do this for the fans, and I think that's the biggest thing."

NEW YORK RANGERS PRESIDENT AND FORMER NHL DEFENSEMAN GLEN SATHER

"It's a pretty complicated question, are we talking spin-o-rama as well? I don't really like the shootout. I think if you're going to play hockey then play the game, play it out, like we do in the playoffs. If you remember, we lost two years ago (2010 season) to Philadelphia in the shootout and didn't make the playoffs, so I would much rather play the game out like you do in the playoffs, because it's just a more true indication of what a team is all about. But the system is the way it is, so that's the way it has to be."

FORMER NHL DEFENSEMAN ROB SCHREMP

"I really like at the end of the game having a winner. The shootout's obviously a tough scenario. There's a lot of pressure on both the goalie and the shooter. I like the system now where you have it during the season, you have the shootouts and then in the playoffs you play out regular because that would be tough to have a playoff series end on a shootout. That's really not a team thing. It's more of an individual thing. I like the system now where during the year you can get yourself in the playoffs by being good in shootouts, but then in the playoffs you have to win it outright and in overtime."

CBS Sports Radio Anchor Peter Schwartz

"As far as the shootout is concerned, I do think it's an exciting part of the game. The crowd is always into it and there is a lot of drama in the shootout. The great part of the shootout is that the superstar isn't always the hero. Many times, a less heralded player thrives in the shootout.

"There's no denying that the shootout is exciting, but I think it may have run its course in the NHL. Maybe they should play a ten-minute overtime and then just end games in a tie like they did years ago."

Hall of Fame Center Daryl Sittler

"I like the current day shootout, obviously there is a winner and a loser. I think the fans obviously stick around and it adds an element of excitement, so I enjoy it. Because of the parity in the league now those points are so important, those teams that win those shootouts, that added point means a lot to the teams as you go through the standings. I think the shootout has created more interest; you see the guys that are shooting are generally the high-profile, well-known players obviously because of their skill, so it just brings another level of excitement for the fans. Certainly it's not easy for a goaltender to be in that situation but overall

I think it's good. I wouldn't want to see a playoff game end that way, but the way the system is in place for the regular season works for me."

FORMER NHL GENERAL MANAGER AND TSN ANALYST NEIL SMITH

"I prefer the old system which had a five-minute overtime with the winner taking all the points. A tie after overtime, would be a tie. This is a fairer way to decide the standings. Moreover, the reward for winning the shootout is one point in the standings which is horribly disproportionate when the reward for playing sixty-five minutes of competitive physical team hockey is only one point if you lose the shootout. I think the effect of the shootout has been minimal during the time it has been in the league. The standings have not been drastically different than if there had been no shootout."

WFAN NY RADIO HOST STEVE SOMERS

"I've gotten used to the shootout after overtime for the regular season . . . I don't think it's hurt the game at all and may make it easier for TV to televise games that won't go on forever, and the NHL needs all the TV it can get."

NY RANGERS DEFENSEMAN MARC STAAL

"I like the shootout. It obviously keeps the standings kind of tight and makes for an interesting playoff race because of those three-point games. I think the only time they lose their luster a little bit is if there becomes too many of them and every once in a while, even though they are exciting, it tends to wear itself out a little bit. But it's always good to look and change the game for the better so in that respect, the shootout is great."

BUFFALO SABRES RIGHT WING DREW STAFFORD

"I like the shootout because it is fun, and it lets you have a chance to decide the game. I'm all for extending overtime a little bit, but from a fan perspective, obviously the shootout is nice. If you lose some shootout points early in the year, it can keep you out of the playoffs. Really, in essence, shootouts are deciding who makes the playoffs and who doesn't."

NY RANGERS CENTER DEREK STEPAN

"I like the shootout, I know a lot of people don't. I know they are testing out a new system this year in the AHL (see below), so I'd like to see how that plays out in certain spots and see how it goes. I know that the guys who did it in The Traverse City Tournament said it was just non-stop action which is pretty cool too. I like how they have switched ends for overtime this year. I think that will really help, but overall I like the shootout. I think it's exciting."

(During the regular season, the sudden-death overtime period will be seven minutes (7:00) in length, preceded by a "dry scrape" of the entire ice surface.

Teams will change ends at the start of overtime.

Full playing strength will be 4-on-4 until the first whistle following three minutes of play (4:00 remaining), at which time full strength will be reduced to 3-on-3 for the duration of the overtime period.

If the game is still tied following overtime, a winner will be determined by a three-player shootout.)

Providence Bruins goaltender Malcolm Subban

"I don't really have a preference. I never played with the pre-lockout so I wouldn't know, but the shootout is pretty fun obviously. It's a little more intense and adds that extra aspect to the game. I think if you look at teams that lost a lot of points in the shootout, it's tough for them obviously. If you asked them, they probably hate it but if you ask a team that does really well, they'd like it. It's biased, you're going to get a biased answer every time pretty much from every team, but for me, I don't mind it. I don't really have much of an opinion on it."

NY Rangers goaltender Cam Talbot

"Shootout or old system of ties? I guess the answer depends if you are coming out on the winning side or losing side of the shootout. I think the shootout is good for the game. The fans enjoy it more. It seems to bring excitement to the game as opposed to ending in a 1-1 tie, but sometimes if you're fighting for those extra points you would think you would rather battle it out in overtime, instead of maybe losing in a shootout, because sometimes it might not be the team that deserves to win that comes away with the two points. It's good for the fans and it's good for the game, and some guys seem to excel in it and others never get to participate in it so that's the other thing. It's not really a full team event, so it does have its upside and downside to it."

NY Islanders center John Tavares

"If it was my choice I would like to see some three on three. I know three on three is something some people see as kind of 'gimmicky' in a way but I think that's the way some people look at the shootout. It's obviously exciting and you get some of the best players in the world in three on three full ice. You're going to see some great plays and some end to end action and more realistic hockey plays will start to decide the games and that's what I would personally like to see, but with the shootout it's nice to have a winner. I think the ties obviously are always tough, but for me I'd rather see three on three or an adjustment in the points system in some way where wins in regulation are more valuable, but certainly I'd like to see the hockey play decide games.

"Teams certainly know that if you have a great goaltender or you have a couple of really consistent shooters, you know with 'Fransy' (Frans Nielsen) we have I think maybe one of the best percentage all time so it gives you a lot of confidence.

New York Islanders star player John Tavares would like to see some changes in the shootout rule.
(Michael Miller (Own work), via Wikimedia Commons)

Whether you're late in a game or into overtime, to know that when you have a very consistent shooter or a really consistent goaltender in that aspect that you really understand that getting there is important because you really don't want to be giving points away in the overtime."

FORMER NHL GOALTENDER STEPHEN VALIQUETTE

"I'm for the current system; however, I'd change it to the 3-2-1 points system like they do in Europe, 3 points for a win in regulation, 2 points for a win in the shootout or overtime and 1 point for the loss. The shootout has definitely brought players into specialized positions, you are going to now want a few guys on your roster that can score in the shootout."

FORMER NHL GOALTENDER MIKE VEISOR

"You know what I would like to see, and this is just off the cuff, but a ten-minute overtime and not sudden death and then go into a different format of a shootout. You take a selected group of three shooters, having them shoot the puck from the hash marks by the face off circles instead of going in on breakaways and the goalie has to stay in the paint. I am looking at it from the goalie's perspective, because I am waiting for the day, with the format they have now, for a goalie to rip his groin like you wouldn't believe. Especially playing all that time, you're a little dehydrated, there's a situation when you get a little dehydrated it causes injury."

FORMER NHL GOALTENDER GILLES VILLEMURE

"I prefer this way (the shootout rule) for the fans. The fans love it, the fans just love it. You ever see people look at their watch to go take their train, things like that, you know make the train, but if there's a shootout, they stay. I love it, I love shootouts, and like I said, you have to be good for the fans, the fans like it, why not do it."

FORMER NHL DEFENSEMAN KURT WALKER

"I prefer the post-lockout shootout for a couple of reasons. First the guys get fired up, especially those that are going to shoot as the competitive edge really makes an appearance. But more importantly it's very exciting for the fans and let's not forget the goalies in this situation, it's time for them to rise to the occasion as well. Overall it's great for the game. Since the shootout rule has been in effect I think it's been very positive overall for all of the teams and the fans. When we look back at the ties, they did play an important role if teams had the same record, ties were counted and considered when it came time to compare records to see which team would go on to play for the Cup. The shootout eliminates that process, you either win or lose so there is no gray area or need to bring ties into consideration."

WASHINGTON CAPITALS RIGHT WING JOEL WARD

"I like the shootout, because I don't take any so it's entertaining for me just to watch.

"The shootout has been entertaining. We get a nice cheering section on our bench, the guys that don't go and it's kind of entertaining for us."

NASHVILLE PREDATORS TV AND RADIO PLAY-BY-PLAY ANNOUNCER PETE WEBER

"I definitely prefer leaving the building knowing there is a winner and that there is a loser. Now I don't know if I prefer this current system as it is right now. I am almost coming of the opinion that I don't like the loser point but if I had to make a choice between ties and leaving with winner and loser, I think I would take the winner and loser. I think the effect on the NHL has been a positive one. It's interesting that the percentage seems to be increasing almost every year of the number of games that are going to the shootout before we get to any sort of decision. I was at the all-star game in South Florida when Dany Heatley was such a star in the game and then won the game in a shootout. Looking around the building that afternoon and not broadcasting that game and seeing how people responded to this, I thought this is one heck of a good idea because no one is being bored by this at all."

FORMER NHL GOALTENDER AND NHL NETWORK ANALYST KEVIN WEEKES

"That's a tough question because I actually played. When I was in the IHL we had shootouts, then the NHL we had no shootouts, and I actually had the last tie. April 4th, my birthday 2004, it was a 6-6 tie versus the Panthers. Luongo (Roberto) and I, so that was the last tie, and then I played after the lockout in the shootout. I'll say this. Shootouts are an amazing way to win, amazing. The fans go nuts especially if you are at home, the guys love it, but it is a brutal way to lose, terrible way to lose, it really is. I like the fact that they are exciting for the fans but rather than the shootout, I'd love to see three on three and re-format the overtime whereby you do maybe a 4-minute four on four, and then you do a 4-minute three on three. I think you would open up the ice so much more which will allow teams to really go for it and really attack and not just have to play safe to get to the shootout. So, for example, depending on what team you are, like the LA Kings, you throw Drew Doughty, Anže Kopitar and Marián Gáborík. If you're the Rangers, you got tons of options too, and you could even throw Ryan McDonagh out there or just three forwards out there depending on your team, so I just know that in practice when you do three on threes, especially full ice, it opens everything up. I think it would really be exciting and you'd still give the fans the excitement and it would showcase the best players. How about Pittsburgh, who they're going to run out there. Evgeni Malkin, Sid and Kris Letang, that would be fun to watch."

Sirius XM host Scott Wetzel

"The regular season shootout is the greatest NHL policy change in the last fifty years. Nobody wants to go home with a tie. Players hate it, fans hate it, everybody hates it. The hockey shootout is like ordering a chocolate cone . . . and getting sprinkles on top. It's an added bonus. The only change I would make is stop giving the losing team a point. I'm an all or nothing guy. The casual hockey fan, which is the lifeblood of any sport, gets a headache trying to read the standings. Two points to the winner, zero for the loser."

Former NHL defenseman Jason Woolley

"I like to relate it to soccer, I am a big soccer fan, I love world cup soccer and for me I would prefer the game to end in overtime and not in a shootout. I think as a player, and a fan of hockey as well, I would like to see a four-on-four then three-on-three before it gets to a shootout, because I would much more prefer to see a goal scored in the regular action of the game as opposed to the shootout. To me that's just way more exciting and it's the way it really should end, but if you get to the shootout as your third tier of the overtime then I am not as against it but I would much rather see a game decided in regulation time. I think the entertainment value for the fans is there with the shootout, but I personally am not a big fan of it. But it is a game of entertainment, and the entertainment value is there, but I do think it is wearing off. I am not 100 percent sure of it, but it has, to me, it seems that it's lost its flare a little bit."

NY RANGERS LEFT WING MATS ZUCCARELLO

"I like the shootout, it gives the crowd excitement and it gets a winner. It's pretty boring to play a game that ends in a tie. I think most of the players like it."

3

NHL Showdown

THE GENESIS OF the "shootout rule" can be traced back to the 1970s, when NBC contracted with the NHL to broadcast professional hockey nationally.

NBC was looking to attract new fans so the network introduced two new features to the telecasts.

The first was "Peter Puck," an animated character in the shape of a puck who explained the rules of the game to those who were new to and curious about the sport.

NBC Sports executive Scotty Connell was responsible for enhancing the intermissions and, along with Tim Ryan, is credited with the creation of "Showdown." The idea may have been fostered by the "One on One" competition that ABC-TV showed during NBA games in 1972—an event that culminated in Detroit Pistons center Bob Lanier's continually backing down Boston Celtics guard Jo Jo White en route to victory.

The NHL's "gimmick" featured some of the league's best players (shooters) who went head-to-head with some of the NHL's best goaltenders in a pre-taped penalty shot event.

Brian MacFarlane, Tim Ryan, and Ted Lindsay hosted the event that featured sixteen episodes. NBC added prize money to the competition that featured sixteen shooters and four goaltenders.

The Chicago Black Hawks had four representatives including goalie Tony Esposito, defenseman Bill White, right wing Jim Pappin and left wing Dennis Hull. The New York Rangers and Detroit Red Wings had three representatives apiece, including goaltenders Gilles Villemure and Roy Edwards, respectively. The defending Stanley Cup Champion Montreal Canadiens were represented by three future Hall of Famers, including right wing Yvan Cournoyer, defenseman Guy LaPointe, and center Jacques Lemaire. The fourth goaltender was Toronto's Doug Favell.

The format of the competition featured two shooters facing the same goaltender in a five-shot match. The shooters scoring the most goals advanced to the second round, while the two goalies with the best save record after the first two rounds moved into the quarter-finals.

"It was real good, everybody enjoyed that, really. It was on every Sunday during the year. It was very, very popular," said Villemure during a recent interview.

The series was taped in October during the preseason in Peterborough, Ontario, Canada, and employed a security system devised to cloak the identity of the series winners, a system which had the added effect of leaving both players and the fans in the dark.

Villemure said, "The way they did it, everybody took five shots and only three counted, nobody knew what was going on. Even if you scored, it didn't mean nothing, or if you missed, it didn't mean nothing."

The pairings were drawn in such a way that no shooter knew the identity of his rival shooter, if he had won or lost, or

Brad Park: "It was the last time I ever had a
drink before a game."
(Steven Carter via Wikimedia Commons)

even which three of his five shots had actually counted for the
competition.

NY Rangers defenseman and Hall of Famer Brad Park was
one of the shooters. "Nobody really knew what was happening,"
said Park. "You didn't know if your shots counted, if they
didn't count, you weren't under the pressure because it wasn't
head-to-head."

"There was no pressure, there was nothing. I didn't know
how much I was making, I didn't know if I won or not, we didn't
know anything," said Villemure. "It was just go in there, try to
stop the puck and that's it."

"You didn't know if you had to score a goal, you knew you
had to score but you didn't have the pressure of knowing that you

were under the gun, that you had to get that goal," Park said, "so when the pressure's not on, maybe the concentration's not on."

NBC made a concerted effort to keep the results private.

Park said, "I understand their need for privacy was paramount, they didn't want anything getting out, they wanted people tuning in to see who was advancing and who wasn't, but like I said, when you were doing your shooting, you didn't know which goalie you were gonna go against, you didn't know whether your third shot, or your fifth shot counted because you had no way to measure it. So it was like, alright, just take the five shots and we'll go from there."

The finalists found out, along with the fans, how they fared when they watched the competition, along with a national television audience, between periods of the third game of the 1974 Stanley Cup Final between Boston and Philadelphia. Neither finalist was a player from either team.

"Every guy is different," said Villemure, "and I knew all those guys, [the shooters] so I knew what they're capable to do."

According to the book *The Rangers, the Bruins, the End of an Era*, by Jay Moran, there were five rounds in "Showdown," with the money values for goals and saves increasing with each succeeding round.

In round one, each goal was worth $400 while each save was $200. By the fifth and final round, each goal and save were worth $4,000.

Villemure had already faced a number of the shooters including Chicago Black Hawks left wing Dennis Hull, the brother of Hall of Famer Bobby Hull, so he had an inkling of what to expect.

The Ranger goalie said, "I knew he wouldn't deke me, I knew he was gonna shoot because he had a helluva shot and I was prepared for him, I was coming out a bit more."

Jim Pappin qualified for the finals after beating Detroit's Mickey Redmond. Both shooters faced Villemure, who had advanced as well.

Villemure allowed one shot to get past him. Pappin scored on his third and final shot after Redmond was denied.

"He [Pappin] was good," said the one-time co-Vezina Trophy winner, "he was a good offensive player."

In the finals, Villemure stopped Pappin's first shot but the second was a goal. When Pappin's third and final shot hit the post, Villemure had won the initial "Showdown."

The goaltender earned $19,700 for the win, while Pappin took home $10,200 (which was nothing to sneeze at in 1974).

To today's sports fans, it might come as a surprise that the NHL and individual teams permitted so many elite players to participate.

"The chance of injury was very little unless you fall down or you're sliding into the goaltender," said Park, "but, it was a thing that NHL approved for promoting the game and the risk of injury was very, very slim."

Park's head coach, Emile "the Cat" Francis, wasn't thrilled with having one of his best players participating in the event.

According to Park, "He didn't necessarily like the time we spent away from the training camp." The competition was taped in one day in a ten-hour session.

At the same time the competition was being taped, preseason games were under way, which led to a bit of an awkward situation for Park. His team, the Rangers, had a game scheduled at Madison Square Garden versus Montreal on the night that his taping took place in Canada.

Park said, "We were flying out of Peterborough on a prop [plane] and on [board] was Villemure, Jean Ratelle, myself from the Rangers; (Jacques) Lemaire, (Yvan) Cournoyer, and (Guy)

Lapointe from Montreal; and (Phil) Esposito and (Ken) Hodge. Once we got on the plane, we asked the pilot what time were we going to get to New York and he said, '7:30.' Okay, great, while the game started at seven, there's no way we're gonna be in the lineup, so we partake of the bar. You know 'Ratty' didn't drink so he didn't have anything, Villemure wasn't playing, he didn't have anything, so myself, Lemaire, Cournoyer, and Lapointe and Esposito and Hodge, we had a very sociable ride back. Esposito and Hodge went on to Boston, the Montreal guys and the Ranger guys got off and went to the Garden."

When Park arrived at the Garden, he was surprised to find out he was playing. "We got there between periods, first and second period, you know, I'd been 'overserved' and they said 'get dressed.' I said 'what do you mean get dressed?' said Park. He says, 'we put you in the lineup.' 'What?'"

"I was drunk as a skunk," said Park.

The Rangers' defenseman dressed and then took the ice.

"Ratelle and I go out and he's sober as a judge and I'm like, 'Woah, I'm woozy,' and everything like that. I get on the ice and I find out that Lemaire doesn't even get out of the dressing room, he's so drunk, Cournoyer and Lapointe, you know we're out there and within five minutes, Lapointe throws up and they take him off and there's Cournoyer and I, you know, just high as a kite, looking at each other, winking, right, and I think my first three shifts, I was minus three. It was the last time I ever had a drink before a game."

The "Showdown" feature was also shown on *Hockey Night in Canada* broadcasts. The event continued in a slightly different format on *HNIC* through the late 1970s, even after NBC stopped broadcasting NHL games. The Canadian version matched four teams, made up of a goaltender (each of whom the teams were named after) and three skaters.

Hall of Fame center Darryl Sittler, who participated in the *HNIC* showdowns as a member of the Toronto Maple Leafs, said he was approached to help with the format. "They had a guy like myself 'cause I lived in Toronto [and] was vice-president of the Players Union and even before in the summertime they would throw out ideas. We were kinda the test guys to see how it would work and what it would look like filming it. Initially, there wasn't a lot to it, there were your shootout shots, but then they had some passing, going through pylons, those sorts of things."

The feature was taped before the season began.

Sittler said, "We taped it in September, before training camp, so most guys are in pretty good shape. It was done in Toronto so for me it was right in my backyard. Then they brought the best guys in from each team and then it was an opportunity to make some money. Like in one year, I think I made ten grand or something; it doesn't sound like much now but back then that was an extra ten grand when you were making sixty, seventy thousand or whatever it was."

The benefit to the players wasn't just monetary.

"From a fan's standpoint, I know, during the season, the fans would look forward to each week when 'Showdown' was part of a series that was on between periods each week building up to the final," said Sittler. "It was good exposure for players who were in it."

Unlike NBC's "Showdown," the participants in the *HNIC* version knew the outcome beforehand. "We knew who won," Sittler said. "The TV people at home didn't because they played each week elimination."

The highlight of these "Showdown" productions was the one-on-one competition between shooter and goaltender.

Penalty shots were something that fans didn't see too often throughout the regular season; so when they were called, it added another layer of excitement to the game.

"It's totally different," said Sittler about comparing a penalty shot in a game to the staged competition called "Showdown." "An in-game penalty shot is meaningful for points on the board for your team right then. [The 'Showdown'] is an individual thing, it's more of a production, a show. We were serious, we wanted to win, we wanted to win some money and then hold the title of being a 'Showdown' champion so to speak. So the guys were competitive."

The Hall of Famer said the competition that he participated in bears a striking resemblance to an event that takes place in today's NHL.

"You take the skills competition that the NHL has around the All-Star Game, it was similar to that, only for us, back then, there was meaningful money on the line—meaningful at the time."

In "Showdown 1978," the goalies were the Los Angeles Kings' Rogie Vachon, Philadelphia Flyers' Wayne Stephenson, New York Islanders' Glenn Resch, and Hall of Famer Tony Esposito of the Chicago Black Hawks. Nine future Hall of Famers made up the shooters' roster, including Montreal defensemen Guy LaPointe and Larry Robinson along with Habs left wing Steve Shutt; Toronto right wing Lanny McDonald, Sittler, and defenseman Borje Salming; Los Angeles Kings center Marcel Dionne; Boston Bruins center Jean Ratelle; and Buffalo Sabres center Gilbert Perreault.

Brian MacFarlane and Howie Meeker hosted the feature that was shown during intermissions on *Hockey Night in Canada* broadcasts.

The competition also featured some all-time greats in an alumni game. Included among the former players were three Hall of Famers: fifty-seven-year-old right wing Maurice "the Rocket" Richard, forty-nine-year-old goaltender Gump Worsley, and fifty-three-year-old netminder Johnny Bower.

Not all the teams were on board with this gimmickry.

Imlach had a "power play" off the ice
with Maple Leaf star Darryl Sittler.
(Ralston-Purina Company, via Wikimedia Commons)

Sittler caught some flak from Maple Leafs General Manager George "Punch" Imlach over participating in the event.

Imlach had been the Leafs' General Manager from 1958 until he was fired in April of 1969.

In July 1979, Maple Leafs owner Harold Ballard brought Imlach back when "Showdown" became a sticking point with his best player.

Sittler said, "I was the vice-president of the Players Union. 'Showdown' had been a series for one or two years. I had participated in it and then the Leafs had hired 'Punch' Imlach as the general manager. He was general manager in Buffalo before that, got fired, then the Leafs brought him into Toronto. My first meeting with 'Punch' was the morning of 'Showdown,' and he called me in his office and he sat me down and he basically said he didn't want me to participate."

The exchange between the captain of the Maple Leafs and the team's general manager turned into a power play off the ice.

"He challenged me to say I was the captain of the team and said, 'You gotta listen to management and do what management says.' And he said to me, basically, 'What would the players on the hockey club think if I let you do what you wanted to do?' My answer was, 'What would the players think if I didn't [participate], because we had a joint venture with the owners at the time, with the players association. I made a commitment, it's the day of 'Showdown.' I participated before, but 'Punch' Imlach was using that as a position of power over me. So when I left that meeting with him, that Friday morning, of the taping for 'Showdown,' I had to make a decision and [also figure out] what 'Punch' was going to do. When I left his office our fourth or fifth line center, Paul Gardner, was in the reception area. So 'Punch' was going to prevent me from going and then he was going to fulfill the [team's] obligation by sending Paul Gardner [instead]."

Imlach despised "Showdown." He went to court in an unsuccessful attempt to get an injunction to prevent Sittler and teammate, goalie Mike Palmateer, from appearing on the show.

"I go up to Markham Arena [in a suburb of Toronto]. It's like, 3:30, 4:00 on a Friday afternoon and all the players are there," Sittler said. "We're at center ice and we're in our NHL jerseys, doing a team picture. And in the middle of the taking of this picture, the trainer came out to the center ice level and says, 'Darryl, Alan Eagleson [the executive director of the NHLPA] is on the phone,' and back then we didn't have cell phones. So I left the team picture, went to the phone, and he said, 'Darryl, the Players Association office was just issued a writ, the Maple Leafs are suing you and they're suing Mike Palmateer if you participate in 'Showdown' with the Leaf jersey on. 'And he said, 'a judge will see it in the courthouse in Toronto at 4:30 that afternoon.' So this is quarter to four, we're on the ice at Markham. At 4:30, the judge would see it and Eagleson asked me if he should go and represent Palmateer and me. So he did that and the judge looked at it and said this is a pile of B-S. There's been an agreement in place, 'Showdown' has been in place, the players are entitled to go."

The confrontation over "Showdown" made front page news in the Toronto newspapers.

Sittler said, "That became a big, big story and a headline in Toronto where basically Darryl Sittler, the captain and vice-president of the Players Union was now challenging 'Punch' Imlach of the Maple Leafs. So I went to 'Showdown' but we couldn't wear our Leaf jerseys."

NHL Showdown 1980 featured five shooters against one goaltender. Participating were Detroit Red Wings defenseman Reed Larson, New York Islanders defenseman Denis Potvin, Washington Capitals defenseman Robert Picard, Colorado Rockies defenseman Barry Beck, New York Rangers defenseman Ron Greschner, and Philadelphia Flyers defenseman Behn Wilson. The goalie was the Maple Leafs' Mike Palmateer.

The event highlighted the skills that make the NHL players so special.

"It was like three-on-three hockey, a defenseman and two forwards," said Greschner.

The competition was taped during the summer and shown during intermissions of the *Hockey Night in Canada* telecasts during the 1979-1980 season.

"It was fun for us," Greschner said. "I don't think anybody ever thought a shootout was going to happen at the end of a game."

4

Shots Heard 'Round the World

ICE HOCKEY HAS been a part of the Winter Olympics since the first Winter Games in 1924. But the sport actually made its debut during the Summer Games of 1920 in Antwerp, Belgium.

The Canadian team was comprised of players from a senior men's amateur ice hockey team called the "Winnipeg Falcons."

The 1920 Games were played at the Palais de Glace d'Anvers (ice palace of Antwerp) and featured seven players per side, instead of the normal six. In the late nineteenth century and the early part of the twentieth century, hockey teams featured a seventh player referred to as a "rover." As the name suggests, this player didn't have a set position but could roam all around the ice.

Canada blitzed the competition and beat Sweden 12-1 to clinch the first gold medal.

The first official shootout in an Olympic ice hockey game took place in the 1988 Winter Games in Calgary. The contest wasn't all that momentous: it featured France and Norway playing for eleventh place. When the teams were tied 6-6 after a ten-minute overtime, France won the shootout on goals from former NHL and WHA right wing Paulin Bordeleau and former WHA Calgary Cowboys center Derek Haas.

It wasn't until the 1992 Winter Olympic Games in Albertville, France, that ice hockey "elimination" games would be decided by a shootout. (The format was added to preliminary round play in 2010.)

The shootout rules in Olympic hockey differ from the shootout rules in the NHL.

Under NHL rules (instituted for the 2004-2005 season), after the first three players shoot, the rest of the active roster has to be used before a second attempt can be made. In the Olympics, five shooters take their turns, and then the same or different players can be used in the "tie-break" shootout.

The first Olympic hockey game to be decided by the new regulations featured a thrilling ending. In the 1992 quarterfinals, Canada played Germany, and after a ten-minute overtime, the teams were tied 3-3.

Both goaltenders played well to set up the showdown. Longtime NHL goalie Sean Burke manned the nets for Canada while Helmut De Raaf, the German goaltender, stopped 33 of 36 shots.

The Canadian team had three goals waved off by referee Seppo Makela and De Raaf made some spectacular saves.

Washington Capitals defenseman Jason Woolley would score the first Olympic shootout goal in the third round. Woolley never thought he would even be part of the shootout event.

"The game had ended and I had come back to the bench and the referee said to Dave King, who was the coach at the time, 'You've got to put together a list of five shooters for the shootout.'

So I started to kind of shift my way down to the end as I figured that there is no chance that I'm going to be shooting, because we had a lot of real good, strong forwards that could put the puck in the net. So I shoved down to the end and sure enough the third name I heard was mine, and I was like, 'What? Did I hear that right?'"

The twenty-two-year-old native-born Canadian was understandably nervous because no one had scored yet in the shootout.

"I knew the game was on CBC and was being broadcast back home, and that was a big deal back in the day of course. But at the same time, it's interesting because you're young and you don't really think too much; you just kind of go do it. Just going to center ice, going down and shooting the puck, I really didn't think too much, and I think that's what helped. Youth helped me at that point."

The Caps defenseman took the puck and went in on De Raaf.

"The one thing I do remember is that I wasn't very good at dekeing at all, but I had an accurate shot, so I knew what I was going to do. I just didn't know exactly where I was going to go with it, but as I got in tighter, he went down into a butterfly and I just went up over his glove. It was kind of a natural instinct for me."

Woolley put a wrist shot past the German goaltender on his glove side in the upper-right-hand corner for an historic tally, the first shootout goal in Olympic history.

"It's the first ever shootout goal in Olympic playoff history, and it would not surprise me one bit that no one knows who scored that goal, especially because it happened so long ago. But hey, for me it's really something I think about a lot and I am very proud of, because, honestly, I think a big reason for that other than time passing is that Eric Lindros scored the winner.

But everyone forgets he actually missed on his first shot. Lindros missed, Dave Archibald missed, then I scored."

Jiggs McDonald and Bill Clement were paired on the TV broadcast and thought the shootout was over after Canada's Wally Schreiber scored in the fourth round.

"We were new to shootouts and there was no producer or stats person or anybody in our ears," Clement said. "The set-up was so primitive for broadcasters from around the world at the Olympics in Meribel [the resort in the French Alps where the Games were held] that we had no safety net. Interestingly enough, Jiggs and I actually counted incorrectly and we both were on the same page—incorrectly."

When Schreiber put the puck in the net, Jiggs made the call. *"Yes, Canada wins! That locks it up. Goals by Jason Woolley and Wally Schreiber, yet Michael Rumrich will take one last shot for Germany."*

Rumrich scored to tie it, which left the announcers a little bewildered.

Being the pro that he is, McDonald was able to "talk" his way out of it and bring the viewers up to date.

"It's a six-man competition, not five as we were earlier on led to believe," McDonald said.

Clement said, "It wasn't any fun after that. We met with Rudy Martzke (their TV critic) from *USA Today* who was in touch with us and everything and it's like, 'Well, you guys blew it.'"

Canada's Joe Juneau missed an opportunity to win it as De Raaf used his stick to poke the puck away. Germany's Andreas Brockmann beat Burke to tie the shootout at two, so at least one more round would be needed.

Center Eric Lindros, who was drafted but had not yet signed with the Quebec Nordiques, made good on his second chance.

Lindros used a pretty deke move to get De Raaf off balance as he buried the puck with a forehand shot to give the Canadian team the lead once again.

After Lindros scored, it was up to Burke to stop Peter Draisaitl, a Czechoslovakian-born center who played in numerous international tournaments with the German squad.

The left-hand-shooting Draisaitl skated in on Burke and unleashed a wrist shot that the Canadian goaltender had to sprawl out in the goal mouth to stop. But did he?

The Canadian team found some luck as the puck squeezed through Burke's pads and was on edge heading towards the net, but somehow, it flopped down on the goal line and never completely crossed.

Following the "hold your breath" ending, Canadian head coach Dave King said, "I think if he would have moved, he would have knocked the puck in. He thought it was caught in his arms, but he wasn't sure. He did the right thing."

"It's not a good way to end a match," said Ludec Bukac, Germany's head coach. "It's better just to keep playing, or even to flip a coin. That's the same thing."

The narrow escape allowed Canada to win the shootout and advance to the semifinals. The Canadians would go on to beat Czechoslovakia in the semis but lose to the Russians (called the "Unified Team") in the Gold Medal game.

Team Canada was well prepared for the shootout as they had practiced it leading up to the game. "That allowed us to maintain our concentration," said Wayne Fleming, an assistant coach for Team Canada.

Even though Canada won, both teams were not thrilled with the way the game was decided. "I'm not a big fan of it," said King, "maybe they should try 4-on-4 for a while and then 3-on-3. At least hockey decides it."

German center George Holtzmann said, "That was the most dramatic finish I have ever seen to an international match."

Lindros was not so kind. "It's stupid," he said.

Fleming felt the shootout eliminated what could have been a very long evening. "If we hadn't had a shootout, we'd be there until tomorrow morning," he said. "That's how well the goalies were playing."

Woolley finished the Olympics with five assists in eight games. The six-foot, left-handed shooter didn't mind playing second fiddle to Lindros.

"Eric was a heck of a hockey player and obviously a big name at the time, and I wouldn't say I was a houschold name by any means. But it was a tremendous experience for me, and a tremendous launching pad for me for my career."

Woolley never thought he would get to participate in the shootout but the head coach believed in him as he found out later.

"It's interesting as I since have had the opportunity to have dinner with my former coach and a lot of my former teammates. I asked Dave King why he chose me. He told me that we had done a lot of shootouts in practice up until the Olympics and he said he was paying attention and that I had a good success rate in practice so he went with me. I guess at the end of the day my type of game [was well suited to the shootout]. I was an offensive defenseman and I was very comfortable in the offensive zone. I wasn't necessarily a scorer per se, but I was an offensive defenseman so I don't think it was ludicrous that he picked me, although it did surprise the heck out of me when it happened."

1994 Gold Medal Game

To have the Gold Medal game in a Winter Olympics decided by a shootout would only add fodder to the constant debate over the merits and credibility of the rule.

In the 1994 Winter Games at Lillehammer, Norway, that scenario became a reality.

After three periods and a scoreless ten-minute overtime, Canada and Sweden were tied at 2-2. The Gold Medal would be up for grabs in a shootout round. Five players from each team would try to score on the opposing goaltender. If the teams were tied, they would go to a "sudden death" shootout round.

Tommy Salo was in goal for Sweden while Corey Hirsch was between the pipes for Canada.

"I hadn't had much success in the shootouts, previously during the year because in Canada we just didn't do them, growing up and all that," said Hirsch, "so I just wanted to put us in a position to give us a chance to, obviously, to win the game."

The twenty-one-year-old netminder from Medicine Hat, Alberta, Canada, felt that deciding the game on a shootout was a disadvantage for the Canadian team.

"If overtime would've kept going, we were starting to take over the game," Hirsch said. "There were some big hits late in overtime that I thought were starting to really wear down the Swedes and I thought if overtime would've kept going, eventually we would've won that game."

Canada's Petr Nedved went first and beat Salo on the glove side with a wrist shot for the first shootout goal. Former NHLer Hakan Loob skated directly in on Hirsch but was stopped on his first attempt.

"I had grown up watching those guys play in Calgary. Hakan Loob had played there. Naslund (Mats) had played in Montreal, so it was just kind of cool to be part of it," Hirsch said.

Canada went up 2-0 after nineteen-year-old Paul Kariya went glove side again to beat Salo. Magnus Svenssion got Sweden on the board as he got Hirsch to go down and then scored from just outside the left goal post.

"You just try and get into a position to make the save obviously," said Hirsch, "and sometimes that's what happens when you're playing against world-class players, they do the right thing at the right time. He's a smart player. At the time you're kinda 'p-oe'd,' but that's just the way it is. You know he made a good play and you just gotta live with it."

On the next try, Salo made a tremendous stick save to deny Dwayne Norris. Hirsch answered, as he came out to challenge Mats Naslund and poked away the puck with the end of his skate.

After the Swedish goaltender stopped Canada's Greg Parks to keep the shootout deficit at one, Peter Forsberg made a beautiful move to deke Hirsch and put a back-hand shot in the net to tie the score.

"I should have had it," Hirsch said after the game. "He just kinda gave himself an out. He waited until the last second, and did a really good job of making sure that I was out of the play before he made his move."

Both Canada's Greg Johnson and Sweden's Roger Hansson, the only participant in this shootout to not have played in the NHL, failed to score so the competition went to "sudden death."

Hirsch said, "I more or less thought that we had a pretty good chance to win, we scored on the first two shots. Really, all we had to do was bury one more and the game was over."

At this point, the coaches could use any player or even the same player again and again to try and end it.

In the "sudden death" round, Sweden went first and went back to Svensson, who'd scored their first goal. Team Canada's goaltender was not concerned with facing someone who had already got one past him.

"I almost stopped the first one, so I felt confident that I'd be able to stop him," said Hirsch. "I wasn't too concerned about him; I felt pretty good about my chances. I thought the first one he had really beat me. I just thought I'd be able to get him on the next one."

Svensson had Hirsch down and missed the net. Hirsch had gotten his wish.

"I preferred that they went first, I just felt that if I could make a save then the game was on someone else's stick, in a sense, where if it's the other way around, then the game is on my shoulders whether or not we win or lose. And at that point, it was just, 'make the save and hopefully we can score after that.'"

Nedved was up next for Canada but he missed the net with a backhand try.

Peter Forsberg has made his stamp in Olympic
shootout history.
(Javatyk via Wikimedia Commons)

Forsberg was up next for Sweden and as he picked up the puck and skated in on Hirsch, he thought about how fellow Swede Kent Nilsson, also a left-hand shot, had scored a dramatic goal in the 1989 World Championships.

The twenty-year-old first round draft pick of the Quebec Nordiques made a move to his left and then poked a back-hand shot past a sprawling Hirsch for the lead. Forsberg had tried the move three previous times in Sweden but he "missed on all three."

Petr Nedved was impressed. "Not too many players go for that kind of move."

Hirsch felt he should've made the save.

"If you watch it, the thing just barely goes under my glove. I really thought I should have had that, [but] it goes under the toe of my glove. I mean, we're talking a matter of millimeters."

The Gold Medal came down to Kariya versus Salo. The Swedish goaltender secured a memorable win when he made a left-pad save.

"The game was won on Peter Forsberg's shot. It wasn't so much [that] Salo made a good save. [He] kinda made a lucky save on Paul Kariya, to be honest," said Hirsch. "The game was won on the Forsberg goal. It was just a great play, just one of those historic moments."

The Swedish team stormed off the bench to mob the winning goalie while the Canadians were numbed by the shock of losing such an epic battle.

That additional goal never came.

Looking back, Hirsch admitted that maybe things could've been different.

"I would've liked to have won, nice to have a gold medal, absolutely," Hirsch said. "I don't lie awake at night thinking about it; we're not making any movies about it. Yeah, I would've loved to have won. Would our lives be different? I don't know. Maybe they would be, but that's the way it ended."

1998 Semi-Finals

The 1998 winter games in Nagano, Japan, featured a shootout in a game for thirteenth place between Austria and the host country. It took eight rounds but the Austrians beat the Japanese team on a goal by center Simon Wheeldon, who played in the NHL for the New York Rangers and Winnipeg Jets.

The '98 Games featured another shootout that was memorable not only for what was at stake, but also because it was the first time that NHL players could participate. This was the result of an agreement between the NHL Players Association

"The Dominator" made a habit of making saves despite being down and seemingly out on the ice in many shootouts.
(Dan4th Nicholas via Wikimedia Commons)

and the International Ice Hockey Federaton. Not surprisingly, every player who took part in the competition played in the NHL, including the goaltenders who went on to become Hall of Famers.

The shootout came in the semifinal game between Canada and the Czech Republic. Dominik Hasek was in nets for the Czech Republic while Patrick Roy was between the pipes for Team Canada.

Canada went first with Theo Fleury who broke in on Hasek but was denied. New York Islanders center Robert Reichel led off for the Czech Republic and he did not waste the opportunity. The left-handed Reichel approached Roy and let go a shot that caught the left post and went in.

"It didn't start well, because the first guy hit the post and it went in," Roy said. "I'm not here to find excuses. If we lose, we lose."

On the next two tries, Hasek made a glove save on Raymond Bourque and then stuffed Joe Nieuwendyk's backhand attempt.

Roy was just as good on his two saves after the goal. The Colorado Avalanche netminder kept the shootout score 1-0 with saves on Martin Rucinsky and Pavel Patera.

The best save of the shootout event came in round four. Team Canada Captain Eric Lindros made a move to get Hasek out of position, but somehow "The Dominator" got his stick on the puck and swept it away, despite being down and seemingly out on the ice.

Jaromir Jagr hit the post on his attempt and then it was up to Canada's Brendan Shanahan.

The Detroit Red Wings' left wing skated in on Hasek and tried to score from a tough angle, but the goalie was equal to the task and made the stop to deny Team Canada and give the Czech Republic an historic win.

After the game, Hasek could only exhale. "Unbelievable pressure," said Hasek, "the biggest pressure of my life. You make one mistake and you lose."

Marc Crawford, Canada's Head Coach, put the game in perspective. "History will say this was a great hockey game. It will go down as a classic. You just wish you were on the other end of the score," Crawford said.

Crawford took some heat for using Ray Bourque in the shootout, instead of Wayne Gretzky or Steve Yzerman. "Ray is great on breakaways," Crawford said. "You go with your gut instincts. We did consider using Wayne." Yzerman took the high road. "I would not second-guess or question any of the guys picked," he said.

It would be the final Olympics for Wayne Gretzky, who won three Canada Cups and a Bronze Medal at the 1982 IIHF World Championships in Finland. This was Gretzky's only chance at a Winter Olympics medal, but he went home empty.

Gretzky said, "There are no words to describe it, the loss is devastating. For me, a Gold Medal was not in the cards for my career."

2014 Preliminary Round

It was billed as the "marquee game" of the preliminary round and it more than lived up to its billing. When it was over, the United States had scored a 3-2 victory in a game that featured an epic eight round shootout and lifted a twenty-seven-year-old from Warroad, Minnesota, onto the "honor roll" of American Olympic hockey.

According to international rules, players are permitted to take multiple shootout attempts after three rounds. That made it possible for T. J. Oshie to take six shots on Russian goalie Sergei

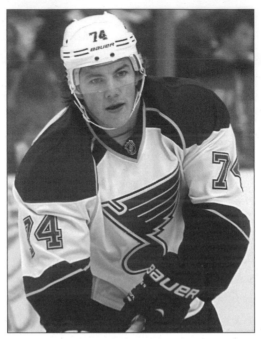

T. J. Oshie usually leaves goalies feeling "Blue" in the shootout.
(Michael Miller via Wikimedia Commons)

Bobrovsky, the final one being the game winner, as the United States won one of the most memorable Olympic hockey games in history.

The game in regulation time offered an aesthetically beautiful display of hockey. "You could just feel the buzz in the air and you just had that feeling the whole game," said Team USA defenseman Cam Fowler, one of the goal scorers in regulation. "It was truly a special game to be a part of."

The game contrasted the styles of the two countries. The American team was using their physicality, while the Russians showed off their marvelous skills, including Pavel Datsyuk's two goals in regulation, the second on the power play to tie the game in the third.

Jonathan Quick: "Playing for your country and
playing in the Olympics is quite an honor."
(Resolute via Wikimedia Commons)

Late in the third, the Russian team thought they had scored
the go-ahead goal but it was waved off. With 4:40 left, Fedor
Tyutin put the puck past USA goaltender Jonathan Quick but
the officials ruled that the net was loose so the goal did not count.

Russian team Captain Alex Ovechkin felt Quick had dis-
lodged the net on purpose. "Nobody touched the net," said
Ovechkin. "Their goalie touched the net and put it out."

Later, the International Ice Hockey Federation issued a
statement supporting the call on the ice. "Upon reviewing the
goal, it was determined that the net had clearly been displaced
prior to the puck going into the net. The IIHF referee super-
visor Konstantin Komissarov confirmed that the ruling that had
been made by referees Brad Meier [an American] and Markus

Vinnerborg was the correct call and that the proper procedure had been followed with regards to the video review."

In overtime, the best scoring chance came when Bobrovsky made a pad save to deny Patrick Kane on a breakaway.

So the game went to a shootout. And T. J.'s moment arrived. He'd been selected for the US team, in part, because of his success in shootouts. Coming into the Olympics, he had a career success rate in shootouts of over 54 percent. Team USA coach Dan Bylsma did not hesitate to take full advantage of those numbers. "I just felt like he was going to score every time," Bylsma said.

The right-handed Oshie went first and beat the Columbus Blue Jackets' goalie through the legs for a 1-0 lead. Evgeni Malkin missed the net on Russia's first attempt and the shootout came down to Ilya Kovulchuk, who beat Quick on the glove side to tie the score and keep the shootout going.

The Russians went first in the fourth round, and elected to use Kovulchuk again. But this time, Quick made a pad save to give Team USA a chance to end it.

Oshie took his second turn and got Bobrovsky down, but he lifted it over the net and the shootout continued.

Datsyuk, who had failed to score in the second round, scored to give Russia the lead in round five, but Oshie was equal to the task as he converted his third attempt, by again going low on Bobrovsky, and putting it between his legs.

In round six, Kovulchuk scored to once again give Russia the lead, but once again, Oshie delivered in the clutch as he tied it. This time the St. Louis Blues center got Bobrovsky down and beat him top shelf.

Datsyuk and Oshie were both stopped in round seven. Kovulchuk was up again in round eight but Quick made a beautiful save to again give Oshie a chance to end it. For the sixth time, Oshie took the puck at center ice and weaved his way though the offensive zone.

When he got between the face off circles, he let a wrist shot go that beat Bobrovsky through the legs.

"I was just thinking of something else I could do to try to keep them guessing," said Oshie. "I had to go back to the same move a couple times, but I was glad it ended when it did, I was running out of moves there."

The crowd of 11,678 inside the Bolshoy Ice Dome, including Russian president Vladimir Putin, were quieted when Oshie's shot crossed the goal line, and US Hockey added a memorable chapter to its history.

Ovechkin sat on the bench for the entire eight rounds of the 2014 Preliminary Round shootout against Team USA.
(s.yume via Wikimedia Commons)

Quick, who has two Stanley Cups on his resumé said, "Playing for your country and playing in the Olympics is quite an honor. It was exciting for the fans and exciting for the players to be a part of it."

Kovulchuk seemed to take the loss in stride. "Nothing terrible has happened," said Kovulchuk, who later left the NHL to play in the KHL. "We played good and showed our character."

Team USA defenseman Ryan Suter said, "It's always good to win."

There was some controversy that surfaced after the game. For some unexplained reason, Russian coach Zinetula Bilyaletdinov chose to keep the leading goal scorer in the National Hockey League, Alexander Ovechkin, on the bench for the entire eight rounds.

The NHL shootouts decide regular season games, but the Olympic shootouts decide much more than a competition. There are sometimes political repercussions that affect the winning and losing country.

In the NHL, Oshie would not have had as many chances to beat the goaltender as the entire roster must be used before any player gets to go twice.

Then again, Oshie would not be playing for a medal in the NHL.

5

Ten Years After

CHANGE WAS INEVITABLE once the National Hockey League resumed play in October 2005 after a labor dispute forced the cancellation of the entire 2004-2005 season.

One of the major changes was the implementation of the shootout rule, an idea that was spearheaded by National Hockey League Commissioner Gary Bettman.

NHL Commissioner Gary Bettman was a driving force behind the "Shootout Rule."
(Courtesy of Mark Rosenman)

"It was something we discussed with the General Managers who tend to be the eyes and ears, the heart and soul of the rules," Bettman said. "Ultimately you need to forge a consensus of the Board of Governors who ultimately have final say on the passage of any rules."

The sport of hockey was on the "lower rung of the ladder" when competing with the other three major American team sports (football, baseball, basketball) so missing a whole season set it back in terms of growing the game and its fan base.

"When we took a year off we were seeking to do things for the game that were extraordinarily positive," Bettman said, "this was something that we thought, consistent with the way we were changing rules of the game and opening it up, it'd be something we thought fans would be excited about."

After seeing how fans were leaving games early in the wake of an imminent tie game, the Commissioner felt the game needed a "shot (or a shootout) in the arm."

"It was clear to me, that over time, pre-shootout, was reaching the point where, the fact, the energy, and the excitement in the building wasn't as good as it was during sixty minutes of regulation," the Commissioner said. "In fact, that reduction in energy seemed consistent with the fact that more people than I would liked to have seen decided that they were gonna beat the traffic because the notion was it was more likely than not, the game was still gonna end in a tie."

Since he began his tenure in February of 1993, Commissioner Bettman has attended many games in person and was heeding the fan's input.

The Commissioner said, "When I had lots of discussions with fans in the buildings I was in, and the fans were telling me, using a variety of descriptive suggestions, that it wasn't very satisfying and that was the impetus."

It took some prodding, but the rule passed.

"There was very little (opposition to the rule) a couple of clubs, more of the traditional, but it was part of the package of all the rule changes," Bettman said, "overwhelmingly I think everybody was excited to be going back to the ice, that the game was relaunching and I think at the time we did it, everybody believed we needed to do something that was emblematic of our desire to come back big, fast, strong and better than ever before."

Coming off a season without NHL hockey, the league felt they needed more exposure than ever before.

In May of 2004, the National Hockey League reached an agreement with NBC on a two-year deal to broadcast regular season games and the Stanley Cup Finals.

The deal was different than previous deals with TV networks as NBC paid no up-front rights fee. Instead the network split advertising revenue with the league after meeting its own production and distribution costs.

The coverage was delayed a year because of the lockout but the league wanted to get more highlights onto all the sports shows that were now being aired and the shootout provided a vehicle to accomplish that.

Bettman said, "Coming back after a year, we had to get people, particularly the Sportscenters of the world and the eleven o'clock news, to show highlights and this was ensuring, whenever there was shootout, there would be ready-made highlights to show during the sports news. That was 'taylor-made' for what we were needing to do as we re-launch."

The 2014-2015 season will mark the tenth year that the shootout rule has been in effect, but there is a sentiment among the General Managers that more games need to end in overtime.

Overtime in NHL games resumed in the 1983-84 season and remained the same until the 1999-2000 season when the league adopted a 4-on-4 format to have more games decided before the shootout. (Beginning with the 1928-29 season, NHL games went to a ten-minute overtime to decide a winner but it wasn't "sudden death" before they were discontinued after the 1942-43 season because of travel restrictions during war time.)

"We went to four-on-four believing that would help get more decisions and having the shootout is fine when you don't settle it by skating," Bettman said, "but the notion is, if we can tweak it a little bit and get a few less 'shoot-it-outs' that'll be fun and even make the shootout more important when you see it less frequently."

The NHL instituted a couple of minor "tweaks" to the overtime rule. Beginning with the 2014-2015 season, teams will not change ends as in the past.

The Commissioner said, "We didn't go to what we thought would be dramatic changes, these were simply 'tweaks' to see if we could move the dial a little bit."

Some unconfirmed statistical analyses are showing 57 percent of the goals in NHL games are scored in the second period, a time when the "long-change" is in effect, a number that raised the eyebrows of the league and the Commissioner.

"We were mindful of that statistic as well," Commissioner Bettman said. "We think it should have an impact."

Additionally, the entire ice surface will be cleaned with a dry scrape prior to the beginning of overtime. Previously, the ice wasn't scraped until before the start of the shootout.

"We think going to a dry scrape to clean up the ice a little bit after sixty minutes should help," Bettman said.

The American Hockey League has "tweaked" their overtime rules for the 2014-2015 season.

Sudden-death overtime will be 7 minutes in the AHL.

Teams will play 4-on-4 until the first whistle following the three-minute mark, at which time, 3-on-3 will play out the period.

Commissioner Bettman was asked if the NHL would consider such a format.

"We talked about it, we'll see if it works or whether it's a gimmick and it's good to have a league like the AHL test those things," Bettman said. "People are saying our game has never been better; I view what we're doing as a bit of a tweak and we'll see what the impact is."

Ten years after, Commissioner Bettman said the shootout has been a success.

"I think it's brought more attention to the game, I think it's brought more attention to stars and I think it's brought excitement to the end games that might otherwise result in a tie," Bettman said. "And all you have to do is look at our buildings during the shootouts, everybody is on their feet."

Under NHL Commissioner Bettman's stewardship the league has grown in leaps and bounds, but the shootout rule may be the most significant chapter of his legacy.

6

The First Shootout

OCTOBER 5TH, 2005, was a banner day for the National Hockey League. The sport made its return to the ice following the cancellation of the entire 2004-2005 season due to a labor dispute.

Center Sidney Crosby, the first overall pick of the 2005 NHL Entry Draft, was making his NHL debut with the Pittsburgh Penguins. So, too, was the Washington Capitals' highly touted rookie Alexander Ovechkin (who scored two goals). And it was the day that the sport itself would be invoking a radical change to the rules.

There was no longer any such thing as a "tie" in the lexicon of the NHL. Beginning with the 2005-2006 season, the shootout rule would be invoked to settle regular season games. It didn't take long for the new regulation to take effect.

On opening night of the 2005-2006 season, in Toronto, history was made. For the first time ever, the National Hockey League had the outcome of a regular season game decided by a one-on-one competition between a shooter and a goaltender.

On October 5th, 2005, Toronto and Ottawa were tied 1-1 late in the third period, so the spectre of overtime and a potential shootout was looming.

With 1:31 left, Maple Leafs center Eric Lindros (who was making his Leafs' debut after signing as a free agent) beat Senators goaltender Dominik Hasek with a wrist shot for a 2-1 lead that sent the sellout crowd at Air Canada Centre into a frenzy. The good feelings were short-lived, however, as Ottawa right wing Daniel Alfredsson scored his second goal of the game, just 29 seconds later, to tie it once again.

The teams played a wide open but scoreless five-minute overtime. This set the stage for an historic moment, as the game would be the first in NHL history to be decided by a shootout.

The goalie matchup for this first ever shootout would be, appropriately enough, a pair of future Hall of Famers as Hasek would go against Toronto's Ed Belfour.

Alfredsson scored the first ever NHL shootout goal.
(Jonathan Milley, via Wikimedia Commons)

In what would become the norm throughout the years, Ottawa, the home team, elected to shoot first. The thinking was if a team could score first, that would put more pressure on the succeeding shooter to answer the goal.

Alfredsson was tabbed to be the first player to have an attempt and he cashed in as he wristed a shot past Belfour's catching mitt for the first ever shootout goal.

Toronto could not use star center Mats Sundin because of an injury. The future Hall of Famer left the game in the first period after being struck in the eye with a puck. Maple Leafs center Jason Allison was chosen to go first for Toronto and the puck was poke checked off his stick by Hasek.

Senators left wing Martin Havlat tried a wrist shot but it deflected off Belfour's stick.

Lindros went second for the Maple Leafs and he missed high over the net.

Before the game, Ottawa left wing Dany Heatley had gone to Bryan Murray to persuade his head coach to use him as one of the first three shooters.

"I was in there (shootouts) in the preseason and I wanted a chance," Heatley said.

The head coach complied. "He suggested to me that he could score," Murray said. Heatley took a cue from Alfredsson's shot and beat Belfour low and to the glove side for the clincher. The Ottawa Senators beat the Toronto Maple Leafs 3-2 in the first ever NHL game that was decided by a shootout.

Hasek was no stranger to shootouts and that may have given him a bit of an advantage. At least, that's how it looked to some of his teammates. "We don't want to get involved in too many of them," said Ottawa center Jason Spezza. "Dom's going to help us a lot. He's pretty solid at it (playing in shootouts), and it's good to get the first one out of the way."

The forty-year-old, who would go on to the Hall of Fame, led the Czech Republic to the Gold Medal at the 1998 Winter Olympic games in Nagano, Japan, and along the way, he stoned Team Canada (including a stop on Lindros) in a shootout.

After the historic game, Hasek said, "I'm not crazy about shoots, but they're always fun if you win, it's a good feeling." "The Dominator" was reminded of his heroics at Nagano but he really didn't want to talk about that event. "Whatever happened six or seven years ago, it's nice memories," Hasek said. "Toronto did not have Mats Sundin. Mats scored two goals against us in the preseason, so you never know what would have happened if he was there in the shootout tonight."

Senators defenseman Wade Redden seemed to be resigned to the fact that the shootout was here to stay.

"It's a new NHL," Redden said. "Two points is two points."

7

The Longest Shootout

IT WASN'T A 15-round fight, but it was 15 rounds that comprised the longest shootout in National Hockey League history.

On November 26th, 2005, the New York Rangers beat the Washington Capitals 3-2 at New York's Madison Square Garden, thanks to a 15-round, record setting shootout that ended on one of the most memorable moves that you'd ever see a player make on the ice.

Unlike Olympic rules, the NHL dictates that every player on the active roster must be used in a shootout before someone can be used twice.

Rangers defenseman Marek Malik, who was not exactly known for his offensive prowess, was the fifteenth man up and he ended the epic shootout with a move for the ages.

The game marked the Garden debut for Capitals winger Alex Ovechkin but it was Malik who stole the show.

Malik scored one of the most memorable shootout goals
as a New York Ranger.
(Resolute via Wikimedia Commons)

While Kolzig was in net for Washington, a rookie goaltender named Henrik Lundqvist was between the pipes for New York.

A first period, shorthanded goal by Rangers right wing Jason Ward made it 1-0 after one. New York went up 2-0 in the second but Caps right winger Chris Clark redirected a slap shot to cut the lead. Then right wing Brian Willsie popped in a rebound to tie it.

The teams played through a scoreless third period and a five-minute overtime to set up the shootout. During the overtime, Washington had a golden opportunity to avoid the new rule.

The bench had noticed that the curvature of Rangers left wing Jaromir Jagr's stick appeared to be illegal. After the referees determined that in fact it was, the Caps were awarded a four-on-three power play. However, they couldn't beat Lundqvist, who made 35 saves.

Ovechkin and the Rangers' Martin Straka traded goals in the first round of the shootout but Washington's Andrew Cassels and New York's Michael Nylander both missed. The teams went scoreless until the sixth round when Willsie scored to give the Caps a temporary lead. Rangers left wing Ville Nieminen answered to send it to a seventh round. A total of fourteen more skaters would fail to score until round 14 when Caps defenseman Bryan Muir fired a wrist shot past Lundqvist.

Rangers defenseman Jason Strudwick then stunned the crowd as he beat Kolzig with a similar move to Muir and there would be a 15th round.

"I'm more upset I didn't stop Strudwick (than I am about the Malik goal)," Kolzig said.

"I started to think it would never end," said Lundqvist.

Caps right wing Matt Bradley began the 15th round and tried to beat Lundqvist with a straight on move, but the first year netminder was equal to the task. Next up was a thirty-year-old who signed with the Rangers as a free agent and was in the first year of a three-year deal. Malik took the puck at center ice and approached Kolzig. The left-handed shooter weaved a bit as he approached the goal and then skated a little to his right to get the Capitals goaltender to commit.

Once Kolzig moved, Malik put the puck between his skates, then used his stick between his legs and flipped the puck, top shelf, over Kolzig.

Like everyone in the barn known as "the Garden," Capitals goaltender Olaf Kolzig was stunned by Malik's skill set. "I didn't expect that kind of move from a defenseman shooting 15th in the shootout," Kolzig said.

The Czech-born defenseman said, "Olie was unbelievable. Everybody tried just about everything possible. Basically, nothing worked. I was in a position where I didn't have to score, so I said, 'Why not?' Maybe that's going to surprise him, and it did."

After he scored, Malik skated back towards the Ranger bench to greet his jubilant teammates and put up his left hand, imploring the crowd to cheer what just happened.

Jagr was awestruck by his fellow Czech. "What a move! With 20,000 people watching you, it's not easy to do that," said the former Capital.

It wasn't until 2013, when the Buffalo Sabres hosted the Toronto Maple Leafs in the preseason, that a game would be extended for so long. That game, too, featured a 15-round shootout. Both Toronto goalie James Reimer and Buffalo goaltender Jhonas Enroth denied 14 shooters each, so the shootout was scoreless as they went to round 15.

Maple Leafs center Jay McClement scored the only shootout goal in the 15th round after Reimer made his 15th save in the competition. Sabres winger Steve Ott said, "At one point I think both refs were just going to call it a draw and kind of pick up the puck and go home and be old-school NHL there for a second and call it a tie."

✳✳✳✳✳

The record lasted a little over ten years until December 16, 2014, when, ironically, the Washington Capitals and Florida Panthers played a 20-round shootout.

The Capitals took the lead in the shootout five times but Florida answered with a shootout goal each time to extend the competition. Florida finally won the lengthy competition on Nick Bjugsted's goal in the 20th round.

8

Shooting Stars

WHAT GOES INTO the mindset of the players who are selected for a shootout? What factors come into play? Do they have an idea of what move they may want to try and execute against a certain goalie? This chapter answers these questions and more, in the words of the skaters who are directly involved.

BRYAN BERARD

How do you prepare for a shootout?

"I didn't prepare myself for the shootout in practice. I didn't think I would ever take one, and I never did, actually I did once. I don't even remember what I tried. I have one breakaway move so I must have used that."

Does having faced a goalie before help in a shootout?

"I think the goalie has the advantage in a shootout. I think goalies prepare for guys who they will face in a shootout and try to remember their past moves."

PATRICE BERGERON

How do you prepare for a shootout?

"There's always moves that you have in your head ahead of time but you try to read what's in front of you, what the goalie gives you. I guess that's the biggest thing for me."

Is it difficult transitioning from regulation to overtime to a shootout?

"Yeah, it's hard. I guess after a while you get used to it, you just have to really refocus and try to really concentrate, stay calm and ready to, if you do get the call, try to make the most of it."

Patrice Bergeron: "There's always moves that you have in your head ahead of time but you try to read what's in front of you."
(Sarah Connors via Wikimedia Commons)

Mentally, is there any difference to when you go in a shootout first, second, or third?

"No, I don't really care. I don't know if I should call it pressure, but if you're first, second or third, your mindset should be the same. It's about scoring and trying to do it for your team so it doesn't change for me, no."

Which is more thrilling? Scoring a game-winning, regular season overtime goal or a shootout-winning goal?

"Regular season OT for sure."

NICKLAS BACKSTROM

How do you prepare for a shootout?

"I have maybe three moves that I am always thinking about, so either one of those. But I think the most important thing I do is I decide before I go out there. You can't make it too hard, you have to simplify it, it might be harder for the goalie."

DAN BOYLE

How do you prepare for a shootout?

"You practice. We did as a team in San Jose and I was one of the shootout guys. You get scouting reports on the goalies and they have tendencies. But honestly, you just have to go out there and figure it out as you skate down the ice."

JOSH BAILEY

How do you prepare for a shootout?

"You kind of really just go with instincts and the goalie that you're going up against. You try not to overthink. In my head, anytime I started focusing on a shootout during a game or during overtime, we usually end up losing in OT. So I think you wait 'till the time comes and you practice here and there. We do practice shootouts and you try different moves but other than that it's going on instincts for me anyway."

Is it helpful to have faced a goaltender before?

"If it's a goalie you have faced more, like an Eastern Conference goalie, you may have a better idea than a guy from the Western Conference where you might not have as good of an idea. But I think more so if you shot against him in a shootout, then maybe you have a better idea and can get an edge."

Do you approach a shootout any differently depending on what number shooter you are in the shootout?

"I don't think so. You go in with the same mindset, trying to score no matter what, so the position isn't all that important."

Logan Couture

How do you prepare a shootout?

"I try to stay as calm as possible. I think about a couple moves before I shoot. I always ask our assistant coach, Jay Woodcroft, for some advice on the goaltender, and then turn on my brain and take what's given to me."

What challenges are presented when transitioning from regulation to overtime to a shootout?

"For me, it's not really that difficult. I just go over my same routine and if the coach tells me I'm shooting, I get ready."

Is having prior experience against a goalie helpful in a shootout?

"It does have an impact a small bit. If I notice the goalie is slow to move to a certain side, or he is playing far out of the blue, I take that into consideration on my shot."

LOUI ERIKSSON

How do you prepare for a shootout?

"You always try to have a couple moves in you and you do it in the practice so it all depends which goalie you shoot at and what you see when you come in and shoot."

Is it difficult transitioning from regulation to overtime to a shootout?

"No, it's not that bad. You are so used to it so it's pretty easy to adjust to it."

Do you prefer to go first, second, or third in a shootout?

"I always like to be the first guy. I don't know why but it just feels less pressure."

Which is more thrilling? Scoring a game-winning regular season overtime goal or a shootout-winning goal?

"The overtime goal."

NATHAN GERBE

How do you prepare for a shootout?

"You practice it enough that you kind of know what you want to do. Goalies' tendencies may change so that you have to study and be ready."

Is it difficult transitioning from regulation to overtime to a shootout?

"No, players embrace that. If you get a chance you get excited for it, you want to be the hero."

Does facing a goalie before help in a shootout?

"It goes both ways. I know his tendencies and he knows mine. It's fun stuff, it's one-on-one, its no other element to it, just trying to score a goal."

Nathan Gerbe: "If you get a chance you get excited for it, you want to be the hero."
(Benjamin Reed via Wikimedia Commons)

CODY HODGSON

Do you prefer to go first, second, or third in a shootout?

"It doesn't make any difference. I'll have a different mentality based on whether we're up or down, the ice conditions, and how I'm doing that game. All that stuff plays a factor, but it doesn't matter to me where I shoot."

Which is better? Scoring an overtime winner or a shootout winner?

"Overtime. In overtime you know it's done (when you score), and it's more of a team play."

DAVID KREJCI

How do you prepare for a shootout?

"I think each guy has a couple moves and you look at who you're playing against, what kind of goalie, so you kind of know what you're gonna do before you actually face the goalie."

Is it difficult transitioning from regulation to overtime to a shootout?

"No, not really. You just wait a little bit on the bench before the overtime starts and same thing for the shootout. It's just a little extra time spent on the bench and nothing really changes."

Do you prefer to go first, second, or third in a shootout?

"I think if you shoot third it's a little bit more pressure because you can either win the game or lose the game, so if you go last it's a little more pressure."

Is scoring a regular season overtime goal a better feeling than a shootout-winning goal?

"A hundred percent. I think overtime has been there the whole time since I grew up watching and the shootout just kind of started [ten] years ago. It's a little more spontaneous I would say."

Brooks Laich

How do you prepare for a shootout?

"You usually have an idea of what you are going to do but you can't put a lot of stress on yourself, you can't worry, you really have to just have fun and sort of lean into it. Don't worry about your upcoming shot or what you're going to do, just have fun with it and relax and just try and make the goalie make the first move."

Is it difficult transitioning from regulation to overtime to a shootout?

"It's not a difficult transition. Regulation is fun, you try and get the win in regulation, and the overtime is really fun, four on four, it's a bit of the wild west there and then the shootout is just a showdown. I've been through many of them so it's not that difficult at all."

Do you prefer to go first, second, or third in a shootout?

"I think most players would say they would prefer to just shoot first, to be the very first guy, it's the easiest I think, but it's kind of fun when you have to shoot and the game's on the line. I've had a couple of those and ended up being successful on a couple of them, so that's very rewarding as well."

Mark Letestu

How do you prepare for a shootout?

"Our goalie coach has a pre-scout of every goalie, maybe some tendencies. We see some video, but it's not something you are consciously thinking about when it's actually time to go. Guys basically have their A and B moves and they go to them whether they work or not, that's why I think most guys are around 50 percent."

Is it difficult transitioning from regulation to overtime to a shootout?

"There's time in between but you're pretty warm at that point in the game. It's not like muscles are going to seize up or anything. The NHL has done a real good job at trying to keep it quick. The dry scrape this year before overtime, that might slow things down a little bit, but with the new rules this year, changing sides in overtime will probably end some more games and we won't have to go to as many shootouts, but for me there really isn't any adjustment that needs to be made physically. Mentally, there is some but nothing crazy."

Do you prefer to go first, second, or third in a shootout?

"Coaches seem to always want to go first, not a lot of coaches when they have the opportunity to choose ever pick second, they must like the idea of putting pressure on the other team. Me, personally, I like to shoot second. I kind of like to know what's at stake, whether I can take a chance with a move, or if I have to go to the 'A' move right away. I am sure goalies watch video just as much as we do and they see what guys are doing, so I would prefer going second as a team but it's not a big determining factor."

Is your approach any different depending on when you go in a shootout?

"First is nice. Just to get out there and if you're the first person to shoot you put a lot of pressure on the other team, hopefully give your goalie a chance to relax and take some pressure off of him. Third is nice too because you sometimes get the chance to end the game. Those are always pretty fun. I prefer going first, though."

Does past experience facing a goalie play a part?

"It definitely has an impact. They are smart guys, they are talented guys, they do their research and they have a lot of pride so if you have beaten them with a move once before, they are probably going to be expecting that same move so you want to keep the look the same but maybe have some alteration to it to keep them guessing. I learned my lesson with [Panthers goalie] Roberto Luongo last year. He made a pretty easy save and made a comment after-wards to the effect that he knew exactly what was coming. So it was a lesson learned for me and you have to keep things fresh because the goalies are watching just as much as we are."

DOMINIC MOORE

How do you prepare for a shootout?

"The best way to prepare for shootouts is to practice them, so you do that whenever you can. You do it in practice this way. When you get into a situation in a game, you don't really have to think about it that much."

Is it helpful to have faced a goaltender before?

"Every time you shoot it's a new time and certainly if you have had success against a goalie that could be a feather in your cap, but it really doesn't count for much when you are going to shoot."

RICK NASH

How do you prepare for a shootout?

"I think you try to have your two or three 'go to' moves. I know we do some scouting before the game because those points are so important. Sometimes it's the difference between getting into the playoffs or not making the playoffs."

Does prior experience facing a goaltender help?

"Confidence is an issue when you're going down the ice. If you have scored on the goalie before and you know what you like to do against him, then you can get him second-guessing himself."

Rick Nash: "Confidence is an issue when you're going down the ice."
(Robert Kowal (Flickr) via Wikimedia Commons)

FRANS NIELSEN

How do you prepare for a shootout?

"I don't do much preparation for the shootout. I pretty much make up my mind as to what I want to do ahead of time. Of course, there are goalies that you have gone up against more that might have an idea of what you want to do, so you might want to change it up sometimes but I don't really prepare for it."

Is it helpful to have faced a goalie before?

"For sure it has an impact. I know there are a lot of goalies who do a lot of studies on the shootout so that gets in your head a little bit too. You don't know if they know what you are going to do, so you know which goalies have done their homework and which have not so you have a feeling of when the goalie may not have an idea of what you're doing."

Does your approach change depending on your turn in a shootout?

"No, but it's definitely a big difference going third. If you have a chance to win the game or lose the game, there is definitely more pressure there if you look at it like that. It's always more fun if you have a chance to go in there to try and win the game on the final shot, so I think that's the only real difference."

Is it difficult transitioning from regulation to overtime to a shootout?

"I always stay focused. I know I'm going to shoot in the shootout so you have to stay in there mentally. I don't think it's that tough. You are playing for big points so you have

Frans Nielsen: "I always stay focused."
(Tuomas Vitikainen via Wikimedia Commons)

to keep being focused even though sometimes it is a little fun once you get to the shootout on the bench. You have to maintain focus, because it's big points out there on the line."

MARK SCHEIFELE

How do you prepare for a shootout?

"You usually do a shootout once in a while in practice, just for fun. When we do that I try to think of moves that I would actually do in a game and try to get the hands going. I think the biggest thing is that you have your moves in place and it depends on the goalie you're going up against."

Is it difficult transitioning from regulation to overtime to a shootout?

"It slows the whole game down, which is a little tough. If you think you're going, you have to keep yourself hyped up and make sure your hands are still in it, because if you go into a shootout cold then your hands don't feel as good as they do during the game."

Does your past history with a goaltender have any effect leading into a shootout?

"Maybe [it affects you] a little bit. Sometimes when you're hot, you're hot. If you have a good record going into a shootout, you feel a little more confident. It's not like if you've missed the last five you feel like, 'I gotta score here . . .' I think it's a matter of putting your last one in the past and having your move ready, your idea of the goalie ready. Then when the goalie comes out at you, you can see your spots and go from there."

ROB SCHREMP

How do you prepare for a shootout?

"Shootouts are a whole different animal. You have about a ten-second window to go down and make a great play and beat a goalie. It's a tough scenario, it really is. You have a short window from when you get off the bench to think about what you want to do and what the goalie does. A lot of teams are doing a lot of research now and studying pre-game. We always had what the opposing goalies' shootouts were and we were shown maybe ten to twelve clips of that night's goalies' previous shootouts. And once you get off the bench you have to run that through your brain and remember what you saw in the video and then try and make your move. It's a pressure situation but once you kind of get used to it, it becomes something you take pride in as that's your way of helping the team, and hopefully getting them that extra point."

Does the shootout order matter?

"It is a big factor. Some people will tell you it doesn't matter. It's a personal preference. When I was in Long Island, I usually went first or second. First is always tough. Personally, I like to go second to see what the goalie's going to do, to see how he is if he is aggressive or if he backs up those types of scenarios, that's why I like going second so I can get a read and then go from there. But it comes down to personal preference. Frans Nielsen was unbelievable. He would go first all the time and he would do whatever he had to do regardless and he would score. He was phenomenal at going first, which then takes pressure off the second and third guy."

MARC STAAL

How do you prepare for a shootout?

"The way I prepare, I undo my bucket, put it up there and sit there and watch. I shot one time, I think it was during John Tortorella's first season [as coach of the Rangers]. I guess he hadn't seen enough of me on breakaways to know better."

DREW STAFFORD

Do you prefer to go first, second, or third in a shootout?

"I like going first, but at the same time there is a little added excitement and pressure when you can decide the game. Really, the order doesn't matter to me."

Drew Stafford likes shooting first in a shootout.
(Michael Miller via Wikimedia Commons)

What is better? Scoring an overtime winner or a shootout winner?

"Overtime, no question. Always."

DEREK STEPAN

How do you prepare for a shootout?

"A lot of times, I don't get picked to go. I'm not much of a shootout guy, so I guess I'm pretty lucky not to be, but we will see. Maybe I'll become a shootout guy. I don't think so [since] I don't have many shootout moves. I just keep it pretty simple."

Does it help to have faced a goaltender before?

"Going into a game, your first thought is, let's end the game before the shootout. But once overtime finishes and then when you get to the shootout, your mindset shifts. I try to stick to one move, try to find something I am comfortable with regardless of who is in net. It comes down to instinct most of the time."

John Tavares

How mentally challenging is it to transition from regulation to overtime to a shootout?

"I think a lot of guys will tell you that in a game, when you get a breakaway, you seem to handle those better than one on one in a shootout. When you kind of have a lot of time to think or the goalie has a lot of time to be set and get ready, you have a lot more time to think about what you want to do. So, at least for me, that's the way it is, but it's part of the game. I wouldn't say it makes a really big impact. I think everyone deals with it and it's been the norm now for awhile."

Does the shootout order matter?

"I think at the time you know that you need to score to extend the shootout or you know you can score to win it. But I think at the end of the day you just try and block out distractions and just focus on what you would like to do to obviously try and score. So that's the way I try and approach it."

Jakub Voracek

How mentally challenging is it to transition from regulation to overtime to a shootout?

"To be honest, I don't really remember. I think I have gone two times in the last three years. I don't even know what goes through my mind. It's exciting as the shootout is always fun for the players."

Is it helpful to have faced a goalie before?

"I don't think it's a big factor, because you are probably still going to go with a move that you are comfortable with. But it also does depend on what the goalie is going to do, whether he is going to come out far from the net, or stay back in the net so you just have to change your mind a little bit on the way to the net."

JOEL WARD

How do you prepare for a shootout?

"We are kind of superstitious, a few of us, so we have to go in order, so usually it's Wilson on the left, I'm in the middle, 'Chimer's' [Capitals' left wing Jason Chimera] on the right, so we try and keep that form there and that seems to be our charm."

MATS ZUCCARELLO

How do you prepare for a shootout?

"Every goalie is different, they all play different, so I just have to try and read the other goalie as much as possible and see what happens. I don't know because every game is different, but obviously if you have a pattern and you stick to that and it works for you, you just stick with that.

Does prior success against a goalie give you an edge?

"I would say it is a factor but usually it's a shooter 'deke.' Certain goalies like [the LA Kings] Jonathan Quick, for example, you know he is going to take away the bottom of the net so most likely you have to go upstairs. So there are tendencies you notice and need to use in the shootout."

9

Inside the Mask

GOALTENDERS ARE THE last line of defense on a hockey team. In the shootout, they become even more important.

Every goaltender has a routine that they go through in preparation for a game; but since the inception of the shootout rule in the National Hockey League, they need to prepare for the possibility of added drama. The transition from regulation and overtime to a shootout can be tricky.

Past experiences can sometimes be helpful to a goaltender in a shootout.

MARTIN BIRON

How do you prepare?

"You will do some shootout drills in practice every once in awhile. Maybe towards the end of a practice you will face some breakaways but there aren't really any drills that can duplicate the shootout, because if you put twenty guys in a line and they come in on a breakaway they might do something crazy or something different. But they might not be the guys that go in a shootout, so there really is nothing that can simulate the actual shootout. Some goalies will watch some video the day before so they can pay attention to what the other guys are doing in the shootout just by watching highlights. Most often goalies just know what other players' tendencies are, so at the end of the overtime they will come to the bench and discuss it with the backup goalie and ask who they think the other team is going to send out, what to watch for. Sometimes the backup goalies have been around a long time and have a little bit more of a book on the players and their tendencies so that's a discussion that usually happens just before the shootout is about to start."

On transitioning from regulation time to overtime to shootout:

"Everyone has their own routines, some guys come back to the bench, some guys take their helmets off, some take their gloves off, some dry themselves off, some drink some water or Gatorade or whatever and then go back in their own zone, hunch over and close their eyes, focus and see themselves. They do a lot of visualization, they see themselves—making the move out of the crease, re-tracking, sliding to the left, sliding to the right, there is a lot of that that gets done prior to the first shooter, while other goalies just like to not worry about going to the bench. They just stand off to the side and wait for the Zamboni pass, and then there are some that like to scrape the crease. It's all personal preference and I have seen it all, but the key is you find something that works, something that makes you feel comfortable and then you stick with it."

Do you remember your first shootout?

"I remember my very first shootout in preseason, the very first preseason game out of the lockout [in 2004]. We did shootouts at the end of every preseason game as a bit of a test and practice, to determine if they were going to use the dry scrape, or just shovel the ice, or do a quick resurface. I want to say the game was against Tampa Bay in my first preseason game, and I remember making a diving poke check against the first shooter which I would never ever recommend now because the players are way too good and the diving poke check really doesn't work anymore. I was not a very good shootout goalie; not that I would pump my own tires, but I was a really good breakaway goalie. If a guy came in on a breakaway in a game I usually did pretty good against him, because the speed was really so much different. But on shootouts for some reason I struggled; I just could never get the right rhythm for it."

Does past experience play a role?

"It certainly does; it works both ways. Players can be very good in shootouts and then go against a goalie who has had their number or a goalie who has had a very successful shootout rate and it makes them change their move and makes them change their setup. So your prior success in the shootout alters how you react to certain things. Some players are really good and as a goalie you're like, man I'm facing this guy. For me it was Jussi Jokinen back in the day, just the fact that his name was on the sheet he already had a psychological advantage because he was so good that he was already in the goalies' mind."

Difference between facing a penalty shot within a game and a shootout?

"A breakaway is a breakaway, a penalty shot is a penalty shot and a shootout is a completely different thing. Those three have to be separated. A breakaway happens in the middle of a game, you can come in on an angle, you can come in straight, you can be at the end of a shift, beginning of a shift, you can have a back check or not, the ice can be bad, you know, so breakaways can have so many variables that it changes the game.

"Now a penalty shot, you take some of those variables out, where the guy might have been at the end of a shift so now he's tired and he goes back to the bench and gets a drink of water. The ice isn't scraped. I always find that the flooding or the scraping of the ice before a shootout changes how a goalie plays. There's a lot more sliding, the puck settles a little bit better for the players. Some players like to go outside of that and that changes how the puck may respond to different things. It's part of the game, you're in the flow of the game. That player might have just had a breakaway so maybe he just did a move, he's not gonna do that move again or maybe he will, so you gotta study that, that's completely different.

"Then in the shootout, you have five, ten minutes to just sit there and think about it. Your team might go first. You might score, whoop, now the momentum is a certain way. They might not score and now you have to make a big save so, the whole transition between your team shooting, the other team shooting is completely different than just having to face one shot, one penalty shot, that's it."

The shooters seem to get more credit in a shootout than the goaltender who makes a big stop. Why do you think that is?

"Well, because I think the odds are in the goalie's favor and you look at the stats, you know, I think that scoring is a little bit more special than making a save, and the way guys are scoring goals. The one guy that maybe was talked about in the shootout was Dominik Hasek, '98 at Nagano, because he made spectacular saves, uncharacteristic saves, laying out, so you remember the Forsberg move. I think it was a one-hander, so people remember that move, people will remember somebody doing a 'spin-o-rama,' that was because they were spectacular moves more than anything else. If the goalie made a spectacular, crazy save to win the game, with flippin' over, legs over his head, glove thrown back and then he caught it, at that moment, I think everybody would be like, okay, that was the save that won it for the team."

Are there any mind games that may take place between shooter and goalie in a shootout?

"If you've had that player's number and you stopped him, that guy might have an 'A' and 'B' move and he might go down the list for his 'D' and 'E' and or 'F' move just because you've been able to stop him, so, there's a lot of 'mental game playing' between players and goalies. Is he a first shooter, is he a third shooter, is he shooting to tie it or is he shooting to preserve a win? There's so many factors that come into play when it's shootout."

For you, who was the toughest to face in a shootout?

"Everybody, they all had my number. I could never stop a beach ball in a shootout. 'Fransie,' Frans Nielsen was hard because of that, because he had that backhand move that was spectacular that you were waiting for because he could bring it to his backhand and go top shelf. On the other side, if you waited too long, he slipped it through your 'five hole' and then you look like a fool, so yeah, I think he was one of the toughest I've faced."

SERGEI BOBROVSKY

How do you prepare?

"I don't really do anything differently in practice for the shootout, I just focus on being the best I can during practice."

On transitioning from regulation time to overtime to shootout:

"It's tough to say how difficult the transition is. It's just as difficult with each change but you have to try and remain focused throughout to try and get your team the two points."

Does past experience play a role?

"For me it doesn't really play a role, I always try to keep to my system and try to focus on my job."

Sergei Bobrovsky: "Staying focused on the two points is key."
(Michael Miller via Wikimedia Commons)

BRIAN BOUCHER

Do you remember your first shootout?

"My first ever shootout, I ripped my groin right off the bone. It was in the preseason coming out of the lockout. We were playing the Minnesota Wild at home in Phoenix and we won the game 3-2. I had played the whole game. Wayne Gretzky was our coach and he had mentioned this right before the game started or it may even have been right before the third period started, that there was going to be a shootout after the game regardless of the score. So the game ends, we win 3-2, and now they are going to do the shootout, just to show the fans how it was going to work during the season. So they flood the ice, put water on the ice instead of a dry cut. The first shooter comes down, he dekes me to my right and I go over to the post and my groin popped right off my bone. I had a 'grade 3 adductor longus tear' and I was out three months because of it. So I certainly remember my first shootout well, so you can imagine why I am not a huge fan of the shootout. Interestingly enough, after that they started doing dry cuts of the ice; I don't know if it was because of my injury. Maybe they just figured there was no reason to wet the ice; If you do a dry cut and clean it up and get the snow out of there it's just as good."

How do you prepare?

"Certainly practice breakaways more. Before the shootout you never really practiced breakaways all that much. Guys like to mess around at the end of practice especially if you are the number two goaltender. You find yourself doing a lot of drills that you don't necessarily want to do, but that's part of your role is to be the 'shooter tutor' for these guys and let them fire pucks at you. If they want to do breakaways then you do breakaways, but certainly after the lockout when the shootout was implemented, you certainly want to practice it a little bit more than you have in the past and some of the guys really, really practice it a lot. I remember seeing Henrik Lundqvist practicing it during warm-ups and he is very, very good at it and it's no secret why he is so good at it. It's because he puts so much practice into it and he has mastered it. Maybe some guys who struggle with their confidence may not want to do it because certainly they can get lit up and hurt their confidence even more, but a guy like him, he practices it even in the game warm-up, which I find pretty interesting."

On transitioning from regulation time to overtime to shootout:

"I don't think anything changes for the overtime. Obviously it can tend to be a lot more wide open in the four-on-four setting so you have to be aware even if your team is skating up ice with the puck and it seems like everything is under control. If they miss the net on a rush or there is a quick turnover that could force a two on one down your throat, things happen a lot quicker in the four on fours. I don't think that your mindset changes other than maybe a heightened awareness to the fact that there could be more odd man rushes in the overtime than in the shootout. I always tried to tell myself and remind myself that I wanted to be out at the shooter to take away the shot to begin with. You have to match his speed coming in. Some guys come in slower, some faster. You want to match that and not back in too fast and then it becomes all about patience at that point, allowing him to make the first move. Those are the things you think about and focus on during the transition from overtime to the shootout and you really don't know who's coming on you. You watch games and see the scouting reports and you try and quickly remember those things as the shooter lines up."

Does past experience play a role?

"No question, if a guy owns me, and he has owned me, certainly I am not feeling confident facing him and anyone that is telling you different is lying to you. The mental side of the game is huge and if a guy has a leg up on you and he has had a leg up on you for some time, there is absolutely no question that when you see him line up you are going to be a bit nervous. Obviously there is some luck involved too. You get lucky that he misses the net, or the puck bounces, but if you have a guy who has scored a lot against you in shootouts or just in regular season, he is the last person you want to see lining up for the shootout."

Rick DiPietro

How do you prepare?

"I always felt that the only way to get better was to practice harder and for me the shootout was no different. It was usually after practice was over that I would take as many breakaways as I needed in order to feel comfortable and confident with my movement and positioning. More repetition with different shooters that all had unique breakaway styles was how I felt I could prepare best for games. I also made a point to watch as many shootouts as I could to pick out any tendencies I saw with the different shooters."

On transitioning from regulation time to overtime to shootout:

"I never minded the transition into overtime. The less time to think, the better. Leading up to the shootout I would go through past experiences I had with the shooters I'd be facing to try and visualize the possible moves they would use and the saves I would make. A shootout was one of the few times throughout the course of a game that a goalie has complete control of the outcome. It's you and the shooter, may the best man win and I liked that."

Do you remember your first shootout?

"My first shootout was a win against the New York Rangers at Madison Square Garden and if I'm not mistaken I saved all three attempts. Not sure there's much more to say. Doesn't get any better than that."

Does past experience play a role?

"Past shootout experiences played a huge role in my preparation. I would take as many mental notes as I could from each shootout that I participated in and also from ones that I watched on television or tape. Most shooters have particular moves and tendencies that will become apparent the more you watch them. It didn't mean that they would necessarily use the same moves every time I faced them, but it was nice to have an idea of what they preferred to do. As much information I could gather on each shooter the better. That extra point was far too important that I would do everything I could to be as prepared as possible."

RAY EMERY

How do you prepare?

"The shootout's a separate part of the game. You know shooters do their homework, goalies do their homework, but you still have to practice. It's an important part of the standings now, the points come in handy and sometimes it makes or breaks a season, so you need to prepare in advance for it and at the same time you really need to understand the importance of it. I think the goalies have the best record at about 70 percent or so, so

I think you just really need to prepare for it, and that starts in practice. Making sure you get your reps in, do your homework, make it as important to you as it really is in the standings."

JHONAS ENROTH

Does past experience play a role?

"I remember the move guys have used when they have scored on me, so I try to make sure I'm not going to give up a similar goal if I see those guys again."

Is there a difference in your mentality between the shootout and a penalty shot?

"Yeah, it's a little bit different. It's a little more nerve-wracking during a penalty shot I think."

Enroth finds penalty shots more nerve-wracking than shootouts.
(Michael Miller via Wikimedia Commons)

COREY HIRSCH

How did you prepare the goalies you tutored as a goaltender coach?

"We practiced the shootout every game day on the backup goalie, so whoever wasn't in goal that night, would face four or five guys. Whoever we were going to use as our shootout guys, they would take three shots each, so the goalie would see typically fifteen shootout-type shots in a practice."

BRADEN HOLTBY

How do you prepare?

"In the past I've just kind of went with it, and react. The clearer the mind the better."

On transitioning from regulation time to overtime to shootout:

"Overtime is harder. Overtime, there is more pressure on the line. It's a four on four situation, you're not accustomed to it, but the shootout you just go with it, you just go with your natural instincts."

Does past experience play a role?

"The thing with shooters is that they usually have more than one move so you don't want to be cheating towards one. That's when they burn you so I just try and see what hand more or less I'm dealt. I like to see what angle they come at me, but as far as a move that they're going to do, I just try and react."

BRENT JOHNSON

Do you remember your first shootout?

"I remember my first shootout in preseason, the first season they instituted them the year after the lockout. I was just trying to catch on with a team somewhere and I was in training camp with Vancouver at the time and remember thinking 'oh my god I am going to absolutely just suck' and I ended up stopping three for three. For some reason, I don't know why, I think it might have even been more than three in the first ones but I could be completely wrong. It was one of those things where I was so, so excited for it, but at the same time, me wanting to prove myself and get on a team."

How do you prepare?

"In Washington there were things that kind of changed with our warm up and I believe they still use the same system. Where they do shootouts kind of like the Rangers do and probably more teams are doing that now, at the end of warm-ups, Lundqvist will take about six, eight, twelve breakaways and I think that's something that has changed. With Pittsburgh we used to do a lot of shootout like drills where guys can kind of come in at their leisure and do what they want and I think that helped me at the time, but on the other hand it's different when you see the same shooter and you kind of know what they are going to do every time. It then tends to go against you a little bit when you have to get ready for the opponents, because those guys are going to do whatever they know works best and truthfully with shootouts, it's all a confidence thing. I've seen guys stop so many in a row and I've seen guys that can't put it together for a shootout. One of the best I ever witnessed in shootout was Marc-Andre Fleury, he's lights out. It's like the most fun thing in the world he can do and he is almost chuckling back there after he makes a save, which I think is fantastic. I never had that personality like he does. For me it was oh my god, these two points are huge and it's on the line, but for some goalies if you have that little thing in you that lets you be that relaxed and that's a great thing."

On transitioning from regulation time to overtime to shootout:

"I think everyone is different when it comes to that. Myself, I was like I didn't want to hear anything. If we had a scouting report, I know some of the guys and obviously what they are going to try and do with their moves. You watch TSN, ESPN how many times, so you get to see Pavel Datsyuk's moves but the thing is that it's different every time. So for me getting a scouting report on someone would really hurt me. I remember my first shootout of my last season was in Edmonton and the guys were giving me scouting reports. I kind of went to the bench during the resurfacing and they are telling me so and so likes to do this, so and so likes to do that. I was like well wait a second, it's 1-1 after overtime, I just had a great game going into the shootout, now I'm thinking about what these guys are going to be doing and I was too much in my head. When a goalie gets something in his head and starts thinking about it way too much, he can get way, way, way off track and that's what happened with me. That was like the first time I had ever done that, so from that point on, I just went to the bench and never spoke to anyone. I just kind of prepared mentally for whatever was going to come down the ice and just kind of react, just read and react."

Does past experience play a role?

"There's a thing that happens during a game situation. If a guy is coming down or he is pushed by a back checker or back checker gets a stick on him on a breakaway, all those things come into play, so I always say to young goalies that I am coaching right now that patience is the best virtue to have for a goaltender. You see the guys that are the best at it, Lundqvist and Fleury. Those guys are so patient. They stay so low and they tempt guys to shoot and they know they have them if they do, but they are also so low and they move laterally so well that patience allows them to wait for that eighteenth move."

On the mental aspect of transitioning from regulation time to overtime to shootout:

"I think being focused is always the most important thing; you have to maintain focus throughout all of it. I'm not sure there is anything you can do or say that changes any of it. As far as the shootout, there is obviously going to be a little bit more pressure on the goalie so they need to be able to deal with that and maintain focus."

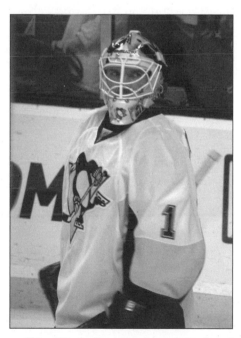

Brent Johnson: "I just kind of prepared mentally for whatever was going to come down the ice and just kind of react, just read and react."
(Dan4th Nicholas via Wikimedia Commons)

HENRIK LUNDQVIST

How do you prepare?

"For me the shootout is a lot about timing and confidence and you work on that in practice. You work to get the right speed and the right timing. If not at every practice, almost every practice I work on it. Maybe not full breakaways, but short breakaways to get my foot speed, and you try to be pretty consistent with that part and keep that going."

On transitioning from regulation time to overtime to shootout:

"You try not to think too much, it's still the same approach, you still need to stop the next shot, obviously it's hard because you know it will be three shots and as a goalie you are a big factor if the team is going to win or not. I always say to win is a great feeling, to lose is the worst because as a goalie you feel very responsible so I think not to overthink it is a big thing, let it take over and don't think about consequences, just stop the puck is my mindset."

MICHAL NEUVIRTH

Does past experience play a role?

"We usually are watching pregame video of their best shooters in shootouts and stuff like that, so you always have in the back of your mind that move he uses the most. For me I'm trying to stay patient as long as I can and 'out-wait' him and have a good position on him the whole time."

Is there a difference in your mentality between the shootout and a penalty shot?

"No. Every shootout is big, and I play every shootout like it's a game seven in overtime so it really doesn't matter."

TUUKKA RASK

How do you prepare?

"Just go out there and try to stop the puck."

Does a shooter's past experience play a role in how you prepare?

"Yeah, we look at a lot of that, their attempts, and obviously everybody has certain tendencies so it has a big impact actually."

What is the difference mentally for a goalie for an in-game penalty shot as opposed to a shootout?

"Depends on the situation. If it's an overtime playoff penalty shot it's a huge difference but other than that, no."

Tuukka Rask: "Just go out there and try to stop the puck."
(Lisa Gansky, via Wikimedia Commons)

Malcolm Subban

How do you prepare?

"I just stretch [laughter]. That's pretty much it."

Is it difficult transitioning from regulation to overtime to a shootout?

"Maybe a little bit. You're in the zone kind of, but it's not too big of a transition I guess."

Does past experience play a role?

"A little bit obviously. If you know a guy's signature move or something, and he knows that you know, he might try to do something else, but other than that it's just reading the shooter."

What is the difference mentally for a goalie for an in-game penalty shot as opposed to a shootout?

"It's pretty similar. With a shootout you have a little bit more time but a penalty shot is just one shot that can really make a big difference in the game. Usually it's called when it's a pretty close game."

Cam Talbot

On transitioning from regulation time to overtime to shootout:

"You have to stay focused the whole game and overtime, so the shootout really doesn't change anything. The only thing that changes is it's only you and the shooter. You just have to stay mentally focused and try not to get too high or too low. If you get scored on you have to get right back up and get ready for the next shot, so not too much changes from the goaltender's perspective."

Does past experience play a role?

"You can't think about it. If you know he has your number you pretty much already have psyched yourself out or maybe you can get a little overconfident. If you think you have his number, you can't get too high or too low in those situations."

STEPHEN VALIQUETTE

How do you prepare?

"You train for it more. After practice everybody would line up at the blue line and take breakaway after breakaway against Henrik, and that's why he dominates in the shootout, because he takes more repetitions everyday than anyone I have ever seen.

For me a lot of prep takes place right before the shootout begins, and getting yourself mentally certain that you're going to stop the puck. When it comes to the shootout I feel that the player with the highest level of certainty wins. It's a mindset. I used to say this to myself: *it's not hocus pocus, it's competitive focus.* You have to get on your toes, you have to hover over the puck, and most importantly you have to have a mindset that you're going to make the save. I truly think that the player that believes that they are going to have the higher level of certainty, that they are going to win that challenge in the end, wins."

Does past experience play a role?

"One of the things I felt I needed to work through is understanding that I compete against the puck. As it moves I move. I had to continue to gain position on it to make the save because if I don't, regardless of who is moving it, 100 times out of 100 the puck is going to go by me because I am not there to get it."

On transitioning from regulation time to overtime to shootout:

"During overtime I think any goalie will tell you, that you start thinking about the possibility of the shootout. As a goalie we are mostly on an island of our own anyway but when it becomes time for the shootout all eyes are on the goalie and doing well and winning a shootout as a goalie is as good as it gets. There isn't a greater feeling of exhilaration in a regular season game. It's as loud as you will hear a home building during the regular season when you win in a shootout, so it's probably the highest level of euphoria you can achieve in a regular season game."

Do you remember your first shootout?

"It was in Toronto, my hometown, and I had to face Mats Sundin, somebody I watched as a child for fifteen years in my home city. I faced him on the second shot and had to make a save against him to win it and we did. I think I did a good job of just looking at the puck and not worrying about who was actually carrying it."

CAM WARD

How do you prepare?

"It's just giving your team a chance. Obviously it's a team game and you need to have your shooters be able to score in order to win, but you also want to give them an opportunity by making some saves. Just not overthinking it, trust your instincts and not make the first move. As we all know, shootout players tend to come in a lot slower than a game situation."

On transitioning from regulation time to overtime to shootout:

"It's definitely a huge difference. A game situation, a guy will be bearing down a lot quicker, maybe feeling the pressure of someone coming down behind him. There's a lot of skilled players in this league who can make some really good moves, and they're all by themselves so you have to be patient."

Does past experience play a role?

"It's kind of one of those things, you love them when you win and you hate them when you lose. Our team, in years past, has struggled and you can't help but think you left points out there. That's the way [it goes]. You try not to put too much thought into it and get ready for the next one, if there is [a next one].

KEVIN WEEKES

How do you prepare?

"You have to work on it and practice it. That's one of the great things about Hank (Henrik Lundqvist) because he is always practicing breakaways, he loves it. A lot of goalies don't necessarily love it, he loves it and has right from the beginning, so if you go to a Rangers' practice, you will see him do breakaways. At the end of pregame warm-up for him, if he is starting, he will do breakaways, so my point is, yeah for me personally, I had to change that and it was something I had to do more of. I had worked on breakaways before but not with as much an intensity and focus that I had after the shootout was introduced in the NHL. Then it became something like 'OK this is something that is kind of important and two points are now on the line,' so it was something I had to tweak in that perspective and work on it even more."

On transitioning from regulation time to overtime to shootout:

"Make it or miss it, very simple. He's going to make it, he's going to miss it. I'm trying to make the save and that's it, that's my mentality. *Make it, make it, make it,* I keep telling myself, my internal dialogue. I'm speaking loud to myself, 'make it.' He's lining up, I'm saying 'make it.' Lining up at center ice is Jeff Carter. We're at the Garden for the Rangers, for example, in our playoff clinching game, he missed it. I made the save and we end up clinching a playoff spot, so that's really what it comes down to. It's having the confidence to really break it down to that. In basketball you heard Michael Jordan say that he wanted the responsibility to take the last shot, make it or miss it, and he programmed himself that he was going to make it, so a lot of it is a mindset. If you channel it that way and you can live with the consequences more often than not, things will go your way."

Does past experience play a role?

"Absolutely. I had Jussi Jokinen when he was with Tampa and I was with the Devils. Jussi came down and he went for his move and I stopped him on it, but sometimes it's hard, because sometimes the guy's going to his move and it's his pet move. You see it coming and sometimes you still don't make the save but more often than not I think it's good to have that 'bank' and that scouting report on him. You know that this guy goes low blocker, I'm going to shade a little bit, maybe I'm going to shade blocker and force him to go glove or whatever it is, it's this whole cat and mouse game. It's like baseball. The ultimate one on one, where a pitcher likes to go high and away, but will he throw high and away? So the batter's in the batter's box thinking he likes high and away so he tweaks his stance a little bit. It's the same constant mental game."

10

Shoot-Outside

ON NEW YEAR'S Day in 2008, NHL history was made—twice. The first ever "Winter Classic" game was played. And it was decided by a shootout.

It was the second outdoor game in the history of the league—in November 2003, the Oilers hosted the Montreal Canadiens before nearly 60,000 fans at Edmonton's Commonwealth Stadium—but the first in the United States when the Buffalo Sabres hosted the Pittsburgh Penguins at Ralph Wilson Stadium.

On January 1st, 2008, a NHL record crowd of 71,217 fans saw Penguins captain Sidney Crosby beat Sabres goaltender Ryan Miller.

The game was played under snowy, windy conditions—typical January weather in western New York. The shootout featured a few differences from a regular indoor game.

First, the Zamboni was not used to clean the ice as would have been the norm in any other regular season game. Second, only one side of the rink was used to conduct the shootout because of the snow.

Sidney Crosby scored the first shootout goal in the NHL's Winter Classic.
(Elliot via Wikimedia Commons)

With the two teams deadlocked at 1-1, Sabres right wing Ales Kotalik was first up in the shootout and the record crowd was on its feet as he took the puck at center ice.

With the "less than normal ice conditions" at the outdoor stadium, Kotalik had a slight problem handling the puck but he controlled it well enough to beat Penguins goaltender Ty Conklin up top for a 1-0 lead in the shootout.

Sabres goalie Ryan Miller stopped Penguins center Erik Christensen to preserve the lead. Conklin then denied Sabres center Tim Connolly and then Penguins defenseman Kris Letang got Miller down and beat him with a backhand flip to tie the shootout round. Sabres right wing Maxim Afinogenov tried for the lead but Conklin did not give an inch and kept the puck out of the net with a sprawling save.

The stage was set for Crosby, the league's brightest young star, to add a chapter to his ever growing resume. The Pens' center took the puck at center ice and started in. Miller came out of the net to challenge the left-hand shooter.

The twenty-year-old held the puck as long as possible to get Miller to commit. After he eluded the goaltender's poke check, Crosby flipped a shot past Miller into the net for the win.

After the game, Crosby reflected on the experience of playing in an outdoor game and then ending it with a shootout goal.

"Growing up, I played a lot outside," said Crosby. "The atmosphere and environment, I don't think you can beat that."

Miller said, "I like facing Sidney. I really want to stop him, obviously. I thought I made a good play to stay with him. I didn't think he made quite the play he wanted, but it worked out for him."

On the first day of 2014, the Toronto Maple Leafs beat the Detroit Red Wings 3-2 in front of a crowd of 105,491 at Michigan Stadium—a.k.a. "the Big House"—a record for any hockey game ever played. The previous record was more than 104,000 for a 2010 NCAA hockey game between Michigan and Michigan State.

It was the first time that a Canadian-based team played in the Winter Classic and it provided the setting for the second shootout ever in the event. The game was played throughout a steady snowfall and a temperature of 13 degrees with a wind chill of minus-1 at game time.

Toronto goalie Jonathan Bernier wore heat packs inside his pants and blocker pad. "My trainer was giving me hot packs, and I put it in my pants as well to try and keep warm," Bernier said.

Unlike the first Winter Classic in 2008, the ice was cleaned this time for the shootout round, although it was done by skaters with shovels, not a Zamboni, and, like six years prior, the teams shot at the same end.

After Detroit's Daniel Alfredsson and Toronto's James van Riemsdyk missed against Bernier and Red Wings goalie Jimmy Howard respectively, Pavel Datsyuk beat the Maple Leafs goalie with a backhander up top for a 1-0 lead. Maple Leafs left wing Joffrey Lupul tied the shootout round as he found the "five-hole" to beat Howard.

The snowy weather was making it difficult on the puck handlers. Detroit center Tomas Tatar was the third shooter but the puck rolled off his stick as he approached Bernier and never got a shot off.

Red Wings coach Mike Babcock said, "The conditions made it so some of the skills in the game were eliminated."

Leafs center Tyler Bozak, who was 8 for 15 lifetime in shootouts coming into his attempt, beat Howard stick side to give Toronto the win.

Bozak scored the shootout winner in the 2014 Winter Classic.
(Michael Miller via Wikimedia Commons)

"Tyler is a player that our coaching staff trusts, pretty simple," Toronto coach Randy Carlyle said. "And when coaches trust people, they put them in situations where you believe the player will get the job done."

It was a memorable experience for the players. Toronto defenseman Jake Gardiner said, "People will ask, 'Did you ever play in an outdoor game?' We can say, 'Yes, we won 3-2 in a shootout.' It's great to be able to say that and just be a part of this whole thing."

11

Shootout to Shoot-In

SINCE THE INCEPTION of the shootout rule in 2005 for regular season NHL games, there have been two instances when a shootout on the final day of the season decided a playoff spot.

It happened for the first time in 2007. The New York Islanders needed a win at Continental Arena against the New Jersey Devils, either in regulation, overtime or a shootout, to beat out the Toronto Maple Leafs for a Stanley Cup playoffs for the first time in three years. New Jersey had already clinched first place in the Atlantic Division but they competed as if their playoff lives depended on the outcome.

Isles right wing Richard Park opened the scoring in the first period knocking in a rebound off a goal mouth scramble to make it 1-0 after one period. After a scoreless second, Park's second goal of the game gave New York a 2-0 lead with just over 12 minutes remaining, but they couldn't hold it.

Devils center John Madden scored twice in the final five minutes of regulation including the game-tying goal (on a power play) with nine-tenths of a second left to force overtime. The score was confirmed by video review.

Islanders center Mike Sillinger had seen things like this before from division rival New Jersey. "What do you do, that's just the way the Devils are," he said. "They never say die."

After a five-minute overtime, the teams went to the shootout. The Islanders' season would be decided by the controversial rule that had been in effect for just two years. The Islanders got a bit of a break because Devils GM and interim head coach Lou Lamoriello decided to rest Martin Brodeur and play backup goalie Scott Clemmensen.

The Devils went first and Zach Parise scored for a 1-0 lead. Then Miroslav Satan tied it for the Islanders.

In the second round, after New Jersey's Brian Gionta had the puck poke-checked away by goaltender Wade Dubielewicz, Islanders center Viktor Kozlov beat Clemmensen "five-hole" for a 2-1 lead.

The Isles had ridden the third-string goaltender to three straight wins coming into the game to put them in position to make the playoffs. Now they needed the 28-year-old netminder to make one more big save.

It was up to the Devils' Sergei Brylin to keep the shootout alive. But once again, Dubielewicz was able to poke check the puck from the left wing to give the Islanders a hard fought victory and a ticket to the playoffs. "I've been waiting for an opportunity like this my whole life," said the winning goalie, "I want to make the most of it."

Isles defenseman Brendan Witt said, "We could've easily said, 'Oh, it's not meant to be,' but guys battled hard in overtime and got us out in the shootout."

Fast forward a few years. With one game remaining in their respective 2010 seasons, the New York Rangers and Philadelphia

Flyers were tied with 86 points and were scheduled to meet in the regular season finale at Wachovia Center (now the Wells Fargo Center).

Two days prior, the Rangers scored a 4-3 win at Madison Square Garden to set up a showdown in the regular season finale. The win culminated a comeback by the Rangers in which they gained ten points on the Flyers in three weeks that enabled them to pull into a tie and set up a memorable final day of the regular season.

"We were stumbling comin' down the stretch. We could have beat them the game before in New York, but we didn't do that," Flyers goalie Brian Boucher said. "I mean I think everybody, I mean if they were placing bets, they hadda been betting against us."

New York scored first. Left wing Jody Shelley tipped Michal Rozsival's shot past Flyers goaltender Brian Boucher for a 1-0 lead

Brian Boucher: "If they were placing bets, they hadda been betting against us."
(Jayne Shives via Wikimedia Commons)

at the 3:27 mark of the first period. (The goal was also Shelley's second of the season, the first coming in the Rangers' 4-3 win Friday night.)

Rangers winger Artem Anisimov turned the puck over in the neutral zone where Flyers center Jeff Carter intercepted it and started a break into the New York zone. The puck sat loose in front of Rangers goaltender Henrik Lundqvist before Flyers defenseman Matt Carle banged home the tying score.

The teams skated through a scoreless five-minute overtime setting up a shootout round where the winner would go to the playoffs and the loser would go home.

Philadelphia was carrying the play for most of the game—after 65 minutes of play, Philadelphia had a 47-25 shot advantage—so the Rangers were pleased to be in the shootout with Lundqvist, one of the best goaltenders in the league.

Boucher had tremendous respect for his counterpart in net and, in a recent interview, revealed that he'd had his doubts about winning the shootout.

"I thought we had no chance, I really didn't," Boucher said. "I mean, I knew they were playing for the tie, you could feel it, you know and they were just playing to get to the shootout and they felt so good about Lundqvist in the shootout."

The Flyers went first and center Daniel Briere made a terrific deke to get Lundqvist out of position and he put it past the Ranger goaltender for a 1-0 lead in the shootout round. Then Boucher made a save with the shaft of his stick on Rangers center Erik Christensen to maintain the lead.

"I knew that Christensen was good in shootouts, he's very underrated in shootouts, he's very good in shootouts. I knew that, so I was really happy with the save I made on him, because he made a pretty good move and shot low-blocker and I stayed with him," Boucher said.

After the Flyers, Mike Richards was denied by Lundqvist, Rangers left wing P. A. Parenteau made a move to get Boucher down. Then he lifted the puck over the fallen Philadelphia goaltender to tie the shootout round at one apiece.

The Philly goaltender was frustrated with himself on the tying goal. "He lost the puck and it screwed me up," Boucher said. "Talk about matching speed, I ended up going back way too fast and it hit my paddle and went up and over me which is kind of unlucky."

Claude Giroux was up next.

"Lundqvist thought he was going 'high-glove' and he kinda opened up a little bit thinking he was shooting 'high-glove' and he put it 'five-hole,'" Boucher said.

It may not have been intentional, but the Flyers' right wing used a wrist shot to beat Lundqvist "five-hole" and Philly had a 2-1 lead. About Giroux's goal, Boucher said, "I never asked Giroux if that's really where he was going. Maybe he missed the shot, I don't know, but I think Lundqvist really thought he was going 'high-glove' there and he fired it 'five-hole.' But I certainly didn't think we had a chance, to be honest with you. I mean Lundqvist is just that good."

It was left up to Olli Jokinen to keep the Rangers season alive. Boucher admitted that he was anxious, knowing what was on the line. "I backed in a little too fast on that one probably just because I was a little bit nervous," Boucher said. "Fortunately, Jokinen didn't make a very good move and I was able to keep it out."

The Finland native tried to slip the puck past Boucher on a backhand but the Flyers' goalie made the stop. Philadelphia was headed to the playoffs and the Rangers were going home. "I'm just so empty, I don't know what to say," Lundqvist said after the game.

On the other hand, the Flyers were justifiably ecstatic.

Boucher said, "It was unbelievable. I mean, I never won a Stanley Cup, but, to be honest with you, the feeling must've been just as good as winning a Stanley Cup."

Boucher said they silenced those who did not believe in the Flyers, including some of their own 'die-hards.' "I don't think anybody believed that we could do it, especially when it got to the shootout, you could just feel it, you could sense it, we had Flyer fans, god I love them, but we had Flyer fans who were sitting on the side of the bench during warm-ups with bags over their heads. But they removed the bags after we won and jumped on board for the playoff ride and we went to the Stanley Cup Finals."

After beating Lundqvist and the Rangers in the shootout, the satisfaction of doing it on home ice in front of the rabid Flyer fans provided a moment that he'll never forget.

"They were about ready to boo us off the ice and we ended up winning," said Boucher. "So it felt really, really good to come through in a clutch moment. It's one of those moments as an athlete you dream about and I know it's, for some people, it's winning the Stanley Cup. Unfortunately, not all of us have a chance to win a Stanley Cup so for me that may have been my best moment, where I could get it done in that setting."

The Flyers made a run to the Stanley Cup Finals but lost to the Chicago Black Hawks in six games. But they made history along the way, by being the first team in NHL history to win a do-or-die game in a shootout to advance to the playoffs.

12

Devil of a Time

DON'T MENTION THE word "shootout" to the New Jersey Devils.

The three-time Stanley Cup winning franchise set a National Hockey League record during the 2013-2014 season as they went 0 for 13 in shootouts. Failing to cash in on thirteen potential points likely cost New Jersey a playoff berth as they finished five points short.

Going back to the 2012-2013 season, the Devils have lost 17 consecutive shootouts. Their last win in the shootout round came on March 10th, 2013, when they beat the Winnipeg Jets 3-2 in the shootout. For the season, New Jersey scored on 9 percent (4 for 45) of their shootout attempts.

Jaromir Jagr, Reid Boucher, Jacob Josefson, and Damien Brunner were the only players to score shootout goals. Patrik Elias was shut out on eight attempts; Travis Zajac missed on his six tries; Adam Henrique and Ryane Clowe had five chances each and failed to score.

After New Jersey lost their final four shootout games in the 2012-2013 season, the streak reached five in early October.

In the second game of the season and the home opener, the Devils lost to the New York Islanders in a shootout, 4-3. New Jersey was 0 for 6 (0 for 12 going back to the previous season) against Islanders goaltender Evgeni Nabokov. Islanders left wing Matt Moulson beat Martin Brodeur in the sixth round to end the drought.

In their very next game in Edmonton, the Devils went 0 for 2 in the shootout and lost to the Oilers, 5-4.

In late October, the frustration of not being able to secure two points in shootout games was already starting to wear on the coaches and the players. "I don't like leaving points on the table like that," said Devils coach Peter DeBoer, "we've got to be better."

Jagr was one of the few Devils to have a shootout goal in the 0 for 13 shootout season of 2013-2014.
(Lisa Gansky (Flickr) via Wikimedia Commons)

One of the greatest goaltenders in NHL history, Martin Brodeur.
(C. P. Storm (Flickr) via Wikimedia Commons)

The Devils added another 0 for 3 in the shootout and lost 3-2 to the Vancouver Canucks in Newark, and now had a futile streak of 0 for 14 in shootout attempts for the season, 0 for 17 overall.

After the game, Elias said, "There's a fine line between winning and losing." Defenseman Andy Greene was more pragmatic. "Some nights, we deserve better, but at the same time, you don't get handed anything in this league," Greene said. "I don't know, we just have to do it. It has to be the guys in this locker room to work to get out of it."

The shootout streak reached four for the season and eighth overall when the Devils lost in Toronto, 2-1 to the Maple Leafs.

To pour salt on the wound, New Jersey's streak of futility within the shootouts reached 0 for 17 for the season (0 for 20 overall) as Michael Ryder, Zajac and Henrique were unsuccessful versus Maple Leafs goalie Jonathan Bernier.

The Devils ended their in-shootout futility but they did not get a win.

In early December, New Jersey hosted the Montreal Canadiens. In the shootout, Devils center Reid Boucher, who was making his NHL debut, scored a shootout goal against Montreal goaltender Peter Budaj, but New Jersey would go on to lose 4-3.

The Devils were now 0 for 5 on the season and 0 for their last 9 shootout decisions.

The final loss of the 2013 calendar year brought the dismal totals to 0 for 6 on the season and 0 for 10 dating back to the previous season, as New Jersey lost at home to the Columbus Blue Jackets, 2-1.

Turning the calendar to 2014 did not mark an improvement for New Jersey as Toronto's James van Riemsdyk scored the only shootout goal in a 3-2 loss in early January. Mid-January brought a 2-1 shootout loss to Colorado.

Seventy days and 24 games would pass before the Devils would play in their next shootout, a 3-2 loss to the Phoenix Coyotes on March 27th. Points were becoming scarce and so were the Devils' playoff chances. Two days after the loss to Phoenix, the team suffered another bitter defeat in the shootout. This time it was at the hands of their bitter rivals, the New York Islanders. Goaltender Anders Nilsson denied Elias and the Islanders had a 2-1 win.

The lack of wins in the shootouts and the failure to secure two points instead of one was coming back to haunt the Devils who trailed a number of teams for a playoff spot.

With three games left in the season, the Devils trailed the Columbus Blue Jackets, the second wild card team in the Eastern

Conference, by three points and were headed to Ottawa for their final road game of the regular season. But once again, they wound up in a shootout. "We need to win," said Devils defenseman Eric Gelinas.

The first four shootout rounds went scoreless before the Senators' Erik Karlsson scored on Devils goalie Cory Schneider. After Dainius Zubrus failed to answer Karlsson's shootout goal, the Devils lost 2-1, had dropped their 12th consecutive shootout of the season and 16th overall, and, as the "coup de grace," they were eliminated from playoff contention.

Devils head coach Peter DeBoer was at a loss for answers to his team's inability to win shootouts. "You don't want to ask, and I have no answers," DeBoer said. He could only lament what could have been. "The effort's there, the preparation's there," DeBoer said. "Their hearts are in the right place. A lot of nights, it hasn't been good enough, for whatever reason, especially in shootouts."

In the penultimate game of the regular season, the Devils participated in one more shootout. But the result was the same. New Jersey suffered its 13th shootout loss and 17th overall dating back to last season after the Devils were beaten by the Islanders, 3-2.

In the shootout round, the Devils missed on all three of their attempts as Nilsson once again "stoned" New Jersey while the Islanders scored on all three of their shots vs. Devils goaltender Martin Brodeur, who was in the penultimate game of his Hall of Fame career as a Devil.

"You should be walking out of the rink feeling better than you do," DeBoer said. "I feel for our group because we shouldn't feel as badly as we do losing two in regulation of our last dozen."

During a radio interview before the 2014-2015 season, Devils President, CEO, and General Manager Lou Lamoriello could not explain why New Jersey could not win a shootout game the previous season. "That's a one-on-one situation, that's not a team planning function. For whatever reason, when we did get the goals in the shootout, maybe we didn't get the save, whenever we got the save, we didn't get the goals. I do not have an answer for it."

The Devils were very successful in the first seven years of the shootout era, going 54-29. Inexplicably, they were 2-7 in 2012-2013. The 0 for 13 shootout record in the 2013-2014 season brings their career record in the shootout to 56-49.

It's safe to say that New Jersey is one team that would like to avoid the shootout round. Lamoriello, who is one of the driving forces behind progressive changes in the NHL, said rule changes— switching ends for overtime, ice scrape before the extra session, no predetermined listing of three players to take part—implemented

Devils GM Lou Lamoriello had no explanation for the 0-13 shootout season record.
(Courtesy of Mark Rosenman)

for overtime beginning with the 2014-2015 season will make the game better.

"The changing of the ends in the overtime will give a little more wide open play—the long change, that is. It statistically shows, the second period, that more goals are scored and you can only attribute to the long change so I think that will help. I think with the new ice with the scrape, the league has done a great job in getting each individual team and arena to get [the dry scrape] done between four and four and a half minutes. I think the future of the overtime will [be] to go to three-on-three, which I'm in support of, after four-on-four which will be experimented in the American Hockey League."

The Devils' streak and failure to secure two points brought to light the fact that the shootout has become an integral part of the regular season and could affect the pursuit of a playoff berth.

13

Who Would You Choose?

LET'S IMAGINE THAT you're the head coach of a National Hockey League team and you're heading to the shootout. You need the two points. Who would you choose to be your shooter and who would you choose to be your goaltender?

NY RANGERS RADIO PLAY-BY-PLAY ANNOUNCER KENNY ALBERT

"I have seen that situation before when the team needed that extra point in the shootout for the playoffs with the Rangers and Flyers when it came down to Olli Jokinen and Brian Boucher. It's a great question because, since the shootout, we have seen some of the greatest players of our time who did not enjoy breakaways and shootouts. Canada doesn't use Wayne Gretzky in the Olympics in 1998. When Jaromir Jagr was a Ranger, at times he did not raise his hand to partici-pate, but if I had to go with one guy I might go with Mario

Lemieux. Just thinking back at some of the breakaways that he converted on during his career. As far as a goaltender there are probably so many of them, but Patrick Roy is the first name that comes to mind because he came up big in big games. You think back to the overtimes in 1993 with Montreal in the playoffs where he was something like 11-0, he made so many big saves in big games when it counted the most."

NEW YORK ISLANDERS CENTER JOSH BAILEY

"Franzie's my shooter no doubt, I'm going with Frans Nielsen. As far as goalies go, I don't know, that's a good question. Obviously I don't know Jaro (Jaroslav Halák) and Johns (Chad Johnson) as much but I always liked having Nabby (Evgeni Nabokov) back there. In practice he was not easy to score on. He is a really smart goaltender but I'd go with one of our goalies now, I'm sure they would get the job done for us."

FORMER NHL DEFENSEMAN BRYAN BERARD

"Comes down to a shootout and I need to win the game, I'm taking Patrick Kane as my shooter because he is the best stick handler without a doubt of any era.

"Dominik Hasek would be my choice for goaltender. His athleticism and flexibility were amazing. No one better on breakaways."

COMMISSIONER GARY BETTMAN (WHO POLITELY AND UNDERSTANDABLY DECLINED)

"The fact is I have such overwhelming regard for all the players who are either currently playing and have played previously and I don't think it's fair to them or to me to weigh in on that. When I'm a fan, I have to keep it to myself."

NEW YORK POST HOCKEY COLUMNIST LARRY BROOKS

"Well, if I needed a save I'd be pretty confident with Mike Richter. I think he was a great goalie on breakaways so I'd be pretty secure with Richter. Taking the shot, put the puck on Joe Sakic's stick. I think I'll have a pretty good shot at winning."

FORMER NHL GOALTENDER MARTY BIRON

"Trying to pick from any era before the shootout is hard because they never had the shootout. A guy could be great on breakaways, and not really carry that through the shootout. I know we had some really good shootout players in New York. We had Erik Christiansen, who was really good, Wojtek Wolski, Mats Zuccarello. I would take Jussi Jokinen of 2006 as my shooter because he was money. He scored a penalty shot goal and a shootout goal in a game against Edmonton and used the same move on both. It was like you couldn't lose, he would always get you that goal.

"For a goalie it's hard to go against Hank because I think he has been very strong. Somehow, someway they ended up losing that shootout to Philly (on the final day of 2009-2010 season) against Brian Boucher. I remember that so well. I was with the Islanders that time and I said if that game ever gets to a shootout the Rangers are going into the playoffs because nobody's going to beat Lundqvist in that spotlight. There's absolutely no way he is losing that shootout and he did, so anything can happen I guess, but I would still go with Hank."

COLUMBUS BLUE JACKETS GOALTENDER SERGEI BOBROVSKY

"For my shooter it's Pavel Datsyuk, because he is so creative and has amazing hands. He is so smart, he can make a good play at any time. For my goalie I would go with Marc-André Fleury, he is so good in shootouts."

FORMER NHL CENTER HENRY BOUCHA

"If the season and my team's playoff lives were on the line I would have to go with Ken Dryden, because without a doubt he was in my opinion, one of the best, if not the greatest goalie in one-on-one situations. He was smart with great anticipation abilities, and was tall and agile to cover the corners. For my shooter I would have to go with my cousin, not because he is my cousin but because he has great hands and the confidence in tight situations to get the job done, so without a doubt I am going with T. J. Oshie."

NEW YORK RANGERS DEFENSEMAN DAN BOYLE

"Well, Martin Brodeur in my opinion is the best goalie to ever play the game so I would want him in my nets. For my shooter, as long as we are going all time, I'd go with a guy who had a pretty good set of mitts, Alexei Kovalev."

FORMER NHL CENTER BILL CLEMENT

"That's easy for me. Dominik Hasek for the goaltender. Dominik Hasek was a human pretzel and a human 'gumby' and very difficult for a lot of shooters to get a read on him. You never knew what he was going to do. He was as unpredictable as a lot of the shooters. For my shooter it's Mario Lemieux. Mario could do things with the puck based on his skill, his size, his reach, his vision, his quickness. I have always said this about Mario. He could do things with the puck that no one else has ever been able to do. On a breakaway his size and his skill and his quickness and his shot and the ability to get the shot off quickly made him able to beat you any way he needed to."

FORMER NHL GOALTENDER RICK DIPIETRO

"I've been very fortunate to face some of the greatest players in the NHL. Mario Lemieux, Pavel Bure, Sergei Federov, Sidney Crosby, but if I needed one shootout goal to make the playoffs I would take Rob Schremp. He was one of the few guys that I've played with or faced that was able to react strictly to what the goalie gave him. There were no tendencies or particular moves that he used. Each shootout was unique and his decisions were based only on what the goalie made available. Always helps when you have some of the best hands I've ever seen. As far as a goalie is concerned there's only one person I would trust to get me that extra point and I'm not afraid to say that goalie is me. This is the exact reason I loved shootouts so much. A goalie's success is largely dependent on the play of his team and there are few times throughout a game that you feel like you are truly in control of your own fate. The shootout was one of them. It's me against you and I know I've put in all the work to be successful."

NBC SPORTS PLAY-BY-PLAY ANNOUNCER DOC EMRICK

"When Marty (Martin Brodeur) was owning hockey, he would be the guy I'd put out there because he used to always entice you to shoot at his glove. He would be waving it and he would try and get you to go there and that was his strength, and he had a very strong record in shootouts. I think Hank (Henrik Lundqvist) overtook him in terms of raw number of wins, but Marty's percentage was quite good. In terms of a shooter probably (Ilya) Kolvachuk. In the modern era it's easy to say (T. J.) Oshie, but back when we were first starting the shootouts, Kolvachuk was pretty deadly."

FORMER 1980 TEAM USA CAPTAIN AND GOLD MEDALIST MIKE ERUZIONE

"For my shooter I'm going to go with Mario. Nothing bothers Mario Lemieux at all, pressure-wise, so it wouldn't affect his approach going in. For a goaltender, as long as it is in any era, and even though the eras have changed drastically for goaltenders, I'd still go with Grant Fuhr. I am a little biased

One of the greatest players of all time, Mario Lemieux was selected by many as their choice to take a season-saving shootout attempt.
(Tony McCune (Flickr) via Wikimedia Commons)

because I know them both well but their personalities are such that nothing phases them and I don't think they would be caught up as far as even being nervous or caught up in the moment and their success themselves as athletes. Grant with the Stanley Cups and what he was able to do and Mario was one of the greatest players to play."

HOCKEY HISTORIAN STAN FISCHLER

"My goalie would be Glenn Hall. He is my favorite goalie of all time because he played 502 straight games without a mask. No one can match that and my shooter without a doubt is the Rocket, Maurice Richard. He was the Babe Ruth of hockey. He could beat you with the forehand, the backhand; he was the one shooter that intimidated the goalies just with his mere presence, before he even started the play. It was like when Joe Louis was the heavyweight champion. He intimidated guys before the fight even started, and that's why I would go with the Rocket."

FORMER NHL LEFT WING NICK FOTIU

"I'm going with Henrik Lundqvist in net, simply because he is the best at it, and Pierre Larouche is the best scorer I ever saw. How many guys could score over fifty goals on two different teams back in the day and almost a third when he had forty-eight with us, so I'm going with Lucky."

SIRIUS XM HOST ANGELO "ZIG" FRACASSI

"There are a lot of great goalies that I would choose, but I'm down to two, Ken Dryden or Dominik Hasek. Dryden because of his height and ability to cover a lot of net. Hasek, since it's controlled chaos with him, as he moved all over the place, with only him knowing what he's doing. Flip a coin and I'll go with 'The Dominator.'

"As for shooters, there are a lot of good choices here. Mario Lemieux, who showed remarkable stickhandling grace for a man his size. Jussi Jokinen, as he specializes in them. However, I'll give it to Peter 'The Great' Forsberg. Anyone who has his shootout move in the 1994 Winter Olympics immortalized on a postage stamp in Sweden, with the move imitated two decades later, Forsberg's the choice!"

FORMER NHL LEFT WING ADAM GRAVES

"I am biased but I would go with Mike Richter because he is my guy, but I would have to say Henrik Lundqvist is right there with him. Hank is fantastic and as you know he has dominated in the shootout for many years here, so he is as good as it gets. For my shooter I'd have to say Mess (Mark Messier). He had a lot of breakaways when he was a player because of his speed, and it was very rare that a goalie would stop him. He didn't play in the shootout era but he was as good as there was when it came down to a one-on-one breakaway situation. I think if you look back at the opportunities he had, he rarely missed, so Mark Messier would be my guy to take the shot."

FORMER NHL GOALTENDER GLENN HEALY

"I would take either Jonathan Quick or Henrik Lundqvist and if I had to choose between the two I would probably go with Henrik, but they are both world-class. For the shooter, I'm going to go with #87. You have to go with the best player in the game, so I'd let Sidney (Crosby) take the shot. There was a certain coach in the Olympics that decided not to use Wayne Gretzky, how'd that work out for him? We didn't even get a medal!"

Former NY Rangers right wing Anders Hedberg

"That's almost an impossible question but I will say this, I wouldn't want to go against Dominik Hasek, because Dominik Hasek was just different, you never knew what he would do in any circumstance. Most other goalies are regimented. If you studied them or watched videos you could find their holes, but with Dominik Hasek, it was always different, so I would go with Hasek. My shooter has to be T. J. Oshie. If you score five out of seven in the Olympics under those circumstances and he was the best in the league last year by far, I'd have to say Oshie."

Montreal Gazette hockey columnist Pat Hickey

"The goaltender I would take, based on the ten years of the shootout, is Marty Brodeur. Now I have no reason to believe he was the best guy in the shootout but I have a feeling he is probably the guy I'd want in there. For the shooter, I'd have to go with one of the two guys in Chicago, either Patrick Kane or Jonathan Toews or maybe Alexander Ovechkin."

Former NHL goaltender Corey Hirsch

"The player I would probably pick would be Mario Lemieux. He was almost unstoppable on breakaways and of course I had the pleasure of seeing that three times in one night at Madison Square Garden, and he went three for three. As far as goaltenders go, I think you have to go with a modern day goalie because the styles have changed so much. There are some goalies that are pretty tough to score on but I would probably have to say Henrik Lundqvist because he's so good at it, but I will say when Pekka Rinne was healthy, before all his hip issues, he was absolutely unbeatable. You could not score on him so I would go with either one of those two."

WASHINGTON CAPITALS GOALTENDER BRADEN HOLTBY

"For the shooter I'd have to go with my all-time favorite Joe Sakic. I probably have to go real old school and go with Terry Sawchuk."

HALL-OF-FAME DEFENSEMAN MARK HOWE

"Wow, season on the line, who would be my goalie? I think I would have to go with Dominic Hasek. For the shooter it would be hard not to go with T. J. Oshie after the Olympics, but I would probably take Mike Bossy."

NHL LIVE HOST E. J. HRADEK

"I think as long as you are asking all-time, I would go with Dominik Hasek in goal because I think in a one-spot scenario of any kind for a goaltender, I probably want Dominik Hasek. As a shooter you want T. J. Oshie. He already showed at the Olympics, in a very incredible spot, that he was just able to continue to do his thing, so maybe that's the guy you want in that situation."

NESN HOCKEY ANALYST BILLY JAFFE

"No doubt in my mind that my shooter is Mario Lemieux. For my goalie I want someone unpredictable. Dominik Hasek, that's who I want because unpredictability seems to be a key to goaltending in a shootout."

Sirius XM NHL Network radio host Mick Kern

"Without a doubt, Patrick Kane. The guy is a human highlight machine, the best stick handler in the National Hockey League. He has proven that he can score goals in any fashion required, and his embracing of a once believed to be extinct old-school skill is breathtaking. I have to admit a goalie does not immediately leap to mind when asked who'd I have between the pipes in a must-win shootout, but after perusing the career stats, I would have to go with Marc-Andre Fleury of the Pittsburgh Penguins. His win percentage is impressive. It might have something to do with the fact he has no time to wander from the net during a shootout."

Former NHL left wing Derek King

"As I'm working for the Leafs/MLSE, I should pick one of our goalies but I think I would go with Carey Price in Montreal and my shooter would be Patrick Kane in Chicago."

Former NHL left wing Nick Kypreos

"I have no issues letting Jonathan Toews take the shot in the shootout with the season on the line, and have no problem with having Henrik Lundqvist being my goalie. I'd feel pretty good with my chances."

ESPN Radio New York co-host and New York Rangers play-by-play voice Don La Greca

"For the goalie it's probably going to be Hank (Henrik Lundqvist). His numbers may not be as good as when he first started but that's probably my goaltender. Guys like Jussi Jokinen were money for a long time, but I really have to think as to whom I'd want. I know it sounds like I'm coming from a Rangers bias, but Mats Zuccarello's actually been pretty good because he is not as skilled as some players. I think the shootout is for those who don't overthink it, so I've always liked him in the shootout, but rethinking it now, game on the line, I would love to have 'The Rocket' Maurice Richard. You just could see his competitive nature in his eyes, so I think he would will the puck into the net."

ESPN.COM HOCKEY ANALYST PIERRE LEBRUN

"I think my shooter would have to be Jonathan Toews. I always remember that 'World Juniors' where he had about a million of them. My goalie would be Carey Price because he seems to be 'zen'-like in those situations."

SIRIUS XM HOST BILL LEKAS

"I'd trust Mario Lemieux as my skater. Lemieux was outstanding in one-on-one situations with the goalie. He had size, but could also come with speed, and had tremendous hands around the net. My goalie would be Henrik Lundqvist. He's done it in pressure situations, including the Olympics. Lundqvist always seems to have a real patience about him. He's got an ability to outwait the skater, rather than committing early, and getting himself out of position."

ESPN HOCKEY ANALYST AND *SPORTSCENTER* HOST STEVE LEVY

"Have to go with Jussi Jokinen as the shooter and Tuukka Rask as my goalie."

New York Rangers goaltender Henrik Lundqvist

"For my goalie, I'd go with Mike Richter. He was a great break-away goalie. And for a shooter I'd say Peter Forsberg."

Columbus Blue Jackets center Mark Letestu

"Bobby's (Sergei Bobrovsky) making the save, I have not seen anyone as good as him in the shootout and I'll go with Peter Forsberg because he has one of the most memorable shootout goals against Team Canada. I mean, they even made a stamp of it. He trademarked that one-handed move, so he would be the guy I go with."

Former NHL defenceman Craig Ludwig

"I guess for me personally Patrick Roy and Martin Brodeur would have to be in the conversation. Not that I'd ever know but it seems to me that the goalies today are better trained goalies. They're bigger goalies, they're harder to score on, so if you were to pick a guy to score on them, I don't know how you could go wrong with Mario Lemieux. I'm going back to when I played against him, so it's different when you played against someone and you know all the things they can do and see some of the incredible goals he scored. I can personally speak to this as I actually climbed on Mario's back, both of my feet were off the ice and he still scored. To this day I still have no idea how he did it. So for me Mario's the shooter. For the goalie, it's hard for me not to go with Lundqvist or Jonathan Quick. I also think of Patrick Roy automatically but I am not sure how good Patrick would be with the current pad size. For me you could throw sixty different goalies in and I wouldn't be able to get one by them, so this is a tough question for me but I would go with Lundqvist. He is big enough, he plays so deep in the net, I just would trust Hank."

Former NHL goaltender Clint Malarchuk

"Jimmy Howard would be my goalie, he's so patient and reads the shooter well, and for my shooter it has to be Mike Bossy."

Former NY Rangers defenseman and radio analyst Dave Maloney

"For my goalie I'm going to say John Davidson and then I'm not going to say J. D. On a one-on-one battle I would be hard pressed not to say Henrik Lundqvist having watched him ten years now and how he competes. He competes on every shot, he battles, so Hank is my goalie. For me, maybe the best one-on-one player skillwise was Pierre Larouche. Donnie Murdoch was pretty good too. Pierre was very crafty. He had an imagination to do different things and soft enough not to have to bowl his way through, so for me I think I would put my money on Pierre Larouche."

NHL on NBC analyst Pierre McGuire

"I would take Mario Lemieux, or Jonathan Toews, but Mario was a guy I won two Stanley Cups with when I was an assistant coach. He was pretty amazing under pressure so probably Mario Lemieux as my shooter. For my goalie, Jacques Plante."

Hall of Fame broadcaster "Jiggs" McDonald

"My goaltender would be Billy Smith only because of his competitive nature. Smitty would do anything it took to stop a shot. I've seen a lot of Frans Nielsen and that backhand shot as well as St Louis's T. J. Oshie. I guess I would go with T. J."

NBC Sports Hockey Analyst Bob McKenzie

"It's easier to pick the shooter than the goalie. I'd go Jonathan Toews. I mean I guess if I was an American I might say T. J. Oshie after the Olympics but I've seen Toews do it time and time again. He's money, as is Oshie. As far as the goal-tender goes, I don't even know who the good ones are in the shootout, but I would always default to a guy like Patrick Roy. I don't even know what his record was on breakaways or penalty shots, but I'd have to go with him."

Sirius XM NHL Network radio host Terry Mercury

"Hate to say it, because he knocked out my guys (Montreal) but that guy Lundqvist, he is deadly on shootouts. I think he could stop just about anybody especially in a big moment. I really would want Henrik Lundqvist in a winner-take-all game, with a nice nod however to Patrick Roy. The guy who I would pick to win it with a goal simply because history indicates that the guy just has ice water running through his veins when it comes to shootouts is Jonathan Toews. Nothing seems to bother him. With all the pressure, every-one in the rink looking at him going back to his junior days when he had those amazing shootouts at the World Junior championships when he scored three times straight, nothing seems to bother this kid."

New York Rangers TV hockey analyst Joe Micheletti

"I'll go with Lundqvist in nets. There's others but I will take my chances with Henrik, because he is as good as anyone out there and he is so patient, which is the key to success in the shootout. As far as who I would want to take the shot, that's a great question because there have been some that have been much better than others over the years. If I have to take one I would have to go with Zach Parise because he has so many different options and so much confidence in scoring and so much of the shootout is having the confidence to do it. There have been a lot of great players in the game, that don't have that, some don't even want to go in the shootout, but give me Zach Parise and I feel pretty good about my chances to advance."

NHL ON NBC ANALYST MIKE MILBURY

"I'd have to say I would go with my guys so I would take Cam Neely as my shooter and for my goaltender right now it would be hard not to say Jonathan Quick. There are so many good goalies through the years, but if we go back to my era, I would have to go with Mike Richter."

NEW YORK RANGERS CENTER DOMINIC MOORE

"I think Hank may have the best numbers of anyone ever in the shootout, so I would go with Henrik Lundqvist as my goalie. For my shooter that's a tough one. There have been guys over the years that have had really high percentages, guys like Jussi Jokinen, but you want a guy who is kind of carefree so maybe Zucc, so Mats Zuccarello is my shooter."

FORMER NHL DEFENSEMAN JAYSON MORE

"My team's on the brink, then my goaltender without question would be Patrick Roy. He was the most competitive

Henrik Lundqvist is the choice of many as their goalie in the shootout.
(Robert Kowal (Flickr) via Wikimedia Commons)

player and consistently gave his team a chance to win. My shooter would be Mark Messier. He thrived under pressure."

OTTAWA SENATORS GENERAL MANAGER BRYAN MURRAY

"I'd go with Peter Forsberg, and for a goalie it would be pretty tough not to pick Martin Brodeur."

NEW YORK RANGERS LEFT WING RICK NASH

"For the goalie I think I'd go with our goalie, Henrik Lundqvist. He's pretty good at them. For a shooter over the years it's been fun to watch Jussi Jokinen. It seems like he only has two moves but they seem to work 80 percent of the time. It's pretty impressive to watch."

Next to Dominic Hasek, many wanted Patrick Roy in the nets for his competitive nature during shootouts.
(Rick Dikeman via Wikimedia Commons)

FORMER NHL CENTER BERNIE NICHOLLS

"Mario Lemieux is my shooter for sure, no question at all about that. Mario was as good a goal scorer if not the best goal scorer I have ever seen. I saw him score five goals in New York one night, a penalty shot, a shorty, a power play goal and two even up. Mario with his reach, he was just such an amazing goal scorer. I just think he was the best goal scorer I have ever seen. In goal Marty Brodeur was the best. No matter who it is I still would give the edge to the shooter, but I guess I would have to go with Marty."

NEW YORK ISLANDERS CENTER FRANS NIELSEN

"Hopefully Halak (Jaroslav) is going to be that guy. I think for my shooter I would go with Johnny (John Tavares). J.T. is our leader so I think it would be great if he was the guy who got the goal to put us in the playoffs."

NHL ON NBC ANALYST EDDIE OLCZYK

"Before this year I probably would have said Lundqvist (Henrik) but since it's an era I'd have to go with Mike Richter. The shooter I'd probably go with would be Denis Savard."

MONTREAL CANADIENS LEFT WING P. A. PARENTEAU

"I have to take Frans Nielsen as my shooter, I think he is the best in the league with his moves and his confidence in the shootout. Zach Parise, Patrick Kane are up there too when it comes to shootouts but I have go with Frans. I played with him and it's pretty impressive what he can do and what he has done in the shootouts so far in his career. For my goalie I might have to go with Jonathan Quick. I am not sure what his numbers are but I have faced him a few times and I have never scored on him. He is so quick and he has a great glove and for me he has been one of the toughest guys to beat one on one."

HALL-OF-FAME DEFENSEMAN BRAD PARK

"For my goalie I am going with a goalie probably no one else is going to pick and that's Gilles Villemure, because we used to do the shootout in practice all the time and his angles were impeccable. He used his stick so well. In practice, if we got two out of five past him you won, and I had a tough time doing that. So I'm going with Gilles. Now for my shooter,

I am going with Mario Lemieux. He is just a pure goal scorer. Gretzky (Wayne) was great but not necessarily a pure goal scorer. With Mario's reach and the way he was able to move the puck from his forehand to his back hand, he would be able to get the advantage of the angle on the goaltender."

New Jersey Devils TV host Deb Placey

"Last game of the season, I need the extra point in the shootout, I'd take Marty Brodeur as my goalie and Jonathan Toews as my shooter. Both of them, ice in their veins, zero nerves under pressure."

New York Rangers TV play-by-play announcer Sam Rosen

"Goaltender-wise, if it came down to a shootout, I might want Dominik Hasek in there, because Dominik Hasek never gave up on any shot at any time. No matter what position he was on the ice he could find a way to keep the puck out of the net whether it was with the glove, his skate, his blocker, his stick he would find a way so I would lean to Dominik Hasek. For my shooter, immediately I would say Wayne Gretzky but he wasn't good on breakaways so I have to take him out of the mix. I would probably go with Mario Lemieux because of the great moves he had and the long reach and he could also beat you with a snap shot. He could come in on you and release so quickly so you probably couldn't tell if he was going to deke or shoot, so I'll go with Mario."

New York Rangers president and general manager Glen Sather

"For my goalie I'd take Henrik Lundqvist. For my shooter, that's hard, there have been so many great shooters over the years but I'd have to go with Mike Bossy. Bossy was a pure scorer, although Mario Lemieux wasn't bad either but Bossy was such a pure scorer. There are lots of guys you could pick. It depends on the particular game, how he's playing, there's a lot of things going on so it depends on so many variables."

WINNIPEG JETS CENTER MARK SCHEIFELE

"Player, I'd probably go with Stevie Y (Steve Yzerman). I just feel like he's the ultimate clutch player. And goalie, I'd probably go with ... Carey Price, actually. I think he's pretty good at that stuff."

FORMER NHL CENTER ROB SCHREMP

"For the goalie I think I would have to go with Dominik Hasek. He was phenomenal. I remember in the Olympic shootouts he was unreal against Canada, he was just so aggressive, he took a lot away and forced the shooter to make a move, so no doubt he is my guy. For a shooter that's a little tougher. Oshie (T. J.) really showed what he can do, you have Toews (Jonathan). I remember that one year Toews and Peter Mueller had that tit-for-tat in the World Juniors. Those guys showed up, but honestly I would take Frans Nielsen. I got a chance to be around him and he scored all the time. He had two or three moves but they worked every time."

CBS SPORTS RADIO ANCHOR PETER SCHWARTZ

"If I was a head coach and I needed one guy to score a goal, I'd probably go with Frans Nielsen of the New York Islanders. He has been practically money in the shootout since coming into the NHL. What has made him good for a number of years is that he's come up with several moves. It's not always the same kind of shot.

"If I needed a goalie to make a big save in the shootout, I think I would go with someone like Ryan Miller, currently with the Vancouver Canucks. He has a big frame and that helps during a one-on-one battle. Even if the skater makes a good move, Miller has that ability to stack the pads and make big saves."

HALL OF FAME CENTER DARRYL SITTLER

"For my shooter, I would have to go with Mario Lemieux because of that long reach, great shot. The goaltender doesn't know what he is going to do, which makes him so hard to defend against, because he just had it all, the long reach, the range, he can move either way, such a highly, highly skilled player. For goalie, maybe back when he was in his prime, Bernie Parent was a pretty good keeper. I think I'd go with Bernie."

NY RANGERS DEFENSEMAN MARC STAAL

"Well, I have played with Hank for seven years now and seen him have a lot of success so I'd go with Henrik Lundqvist in goal. And for a shooter, there are so many good ones but Zucc's money, so I'd go with Mats Zuccarello."

NEW YORK RANGERS CENTER DEREK STEPAN

"I like Henrik Lundqvist a lot for my goalie and for my shooter, I'm going to go with another one of my teammates and go with Zucc. I like Mats Zuccarello's hands in the shootout."

NEW YORK ISLANDERS CENTER JOHN TAVARES

"I would probably pick Mario Lemieux. I remember watching his highlights as a kid and goalies couldn't stop that reach. He had that reach that was undeniable. I think Dominik Hasek or Patrick Roy for goal but I would probably take Hasek. I remember what he did in '88 in the Olympics and he was just so unpredictable, you never knew what he was going to do."

FORMER NHL GOALTENDER GILLES VILLEMURE

"That is a tough question, but I'd have to go with a guy like Jean Ratelle. He had a very, very good wrist shot and he could handle the puck very well, of course, because he was a 'center-man' so I would go with him or, believe it or not, Brad Park because he was real good with the puck. Rod Gilbert and Vic Hadfield, too, but I'd stick with Jean. For the guy who I would want to make the stop, in my era, there were so many great goaltenders, every one of them were so good, there were only twelve teams but if I had to pick one it would be Eddie Giacomin, of course."

WASHINGTON CAPITALS RIGHT WING JOEL WARD

"For the shooter, I'm going with 1994 Alexander Mogilny, and for the goalie, I'm going with 1993 Eddie Belfour!"

NASHVILLE PREDATORS PLAY-BY-PLAY ANNOUNCER PETE WEBER

"If I need the goal and I can bring back anyone I want, I would go with the guy I saw execute the best in the shootout and that was Paul Kariya. I am going to go with a money goaltender and I would be very, very happy and confident because when you come right down to it and you need to stop a big shot, it would have to be Gerry Cheevers."

FORMER NHL GOALTENDER KEVIN WEEKES

"As far as a shooter, I'd have to go with Jonathan Toews or Patrick Kane because all those Chicago cats do is deliver. I would say as far as a goalie, I would have Hasek and Hank (Henrik Lundqvist) because he is excellent in the shootouts. That's the ilk that I consider Hank in, that's the grouping that he is on par with, and that's where he is trending. If you look at his numbers and all his accomplishments, he is a future Hall of Famer."

SIRIUS XM HOST SCOTT WETZEL

"You could make this chapter one sentence if you really wanted to. How could anyone argue putting the puck on anybody else's stick other than the greatest player of all time, Wayne Gretzky?

"Could you imagine a goalie's nerves knowing the greatest hockey player of all time is coming at him with Gretzky's season on the line? Gretzky versus Roy, Gretzky versus Brodeur, Gretzky versus any of the greats. It's no match. The 'Great One' would score nearly every time."

14

The Fan's Corner

Anaheim Ducks

KEN "TOE" BLAKE

"I have been a fan of the Anaheim Ducks for the past fifteen years.

"I definitely prefer the pre-lockout system as it is a true indicator of a team's ability rather than going to a shootout where an individual's effort is always rewarded. To sum it all up, I do not like the shootout at all!

"If I had to pick a shooter and goalie from any of the Ducks players, I would have to choose Paul Kariya and Jean-Sebastien Giguere. I'd go with Kariya in his youth (having a slight edge over everybody's favorite Teemu Selanne) as I feel he was the most exciting player of any era. I'd go with Giguere as my goalie as not only did he backstop us to a Stanley Cup in 2007, but was also the Conn Smythe winner when the Ducks lost to the Devils in the 2003 Final."

Arizona Coyotes

Katrina DeVinny

"I have been a fan of the Arizona Coyotes since their transfer from Winnipeg in 1996!

"I prefer the post lockout system using the shootout. It is also a nice chance to see the skill of the goaltenders as well as the skills of some very talented marksmen.

"If the Coyotes' playoff chances came down to a shootout, the one shooter I would choose would be Mikkel Boedker. He is one of the best goal scorers the Coyotes have. The goalie I would select would be 'The Boolin Wall' Nikolai Khabibulin. He was a Coyote from 1996 till 1999. He was a great goaltender in one-on-one situations and I would trust him in net during a shootout."

Boston Bruins

William Watson

"I have been a Bruins fan since 1976 and I like the pre-lockout system of ties. Love to see a breakaway, but not a minimum of six at the end of a game. Takes away from how special it is.

"If the Bruins' season came down to a shootout and I could take any goalie in franchise history, it would have to be Gerry Cheevers. He was aggressive and not afraid to go after the puck, no matter what traffic was out in front of him.

"To take the shot, I will choose Adam Oates. He scored goals in pressure situations and stayed cool in the process."

Buffalo Sabres

RICH KALLEY

"I have been a Sabres Fan since 1991.

"Having played as a goaltender for about ten years, I can honestly say I prefer the pre-lockout system of games being able to end in a tie.

"If the Sabres' season came down to a shootout and I could take any goalie in franchise history, it would be Grant Fuhr . . . hands down. As far as the shooter is concerned, I would go with Rick Martin. He was small and fast with a very good touch. One of those guys who the game seemed to slow down for."

Calgary Flames

BREANNA STANGELAND

"I have been a Calgary Flames Fan for twelve years.

"I'm not a fan of the game ending in a tie. Shootouts will keep you on the edge of your seat and glued to the game. Until a better solution is arranged, I'll support the shootout.

"If the season came down to a shootout, it would be Miikka Kiprusoff. He helped lead the Calgary Flames to the Stanley Cup final in the 2003-04 season.

"For the shooter I would pick Jarome Iginla. He is not only one of the best players the Calgary Flames have ever had, but one of the best the league has ever seen. Iginla is definitely my #1 choice to be a shooter."

Carolina Hurricanes

GABE CORNWALL

"I have been a Carolina Hurricanes fan since the then-Entertainment and Sports Arena opened in Raleigh in 1999.

"While I'm not the biggest fan of the shootout, better that than skating around for five minutes, having no one score and declaring a tie.

"Given the relatively short history of the Hurricanes, certainly compared to an Original Six market, the shootout goalie for the Carolina Hurricanes has to be Cam Ward. His first game in goal in the NHL was the Hurricanes' opener in the 2005-06 season. Yup, the second game to feature the shootout following the season-long lockout and rules changes.

"Ward stopped Mario Lemieux and Ziggy Palffy in the first two rounds and finished by stopping eighteen-year-old Sidney Crosby in the third round to lock up the victory.

"The shooter has to be Jussi Jokinen, who is noted for a high shootout percentage."

Chicago Blackhawks

Jacob Levenfeld

"I have been a lifetime 'Hawks fan, but die-hard day-to-day fan for twelve years.

"The shootout allows a team to showcase its offensive superstars and top goaltenders, but a shootout victory is not a team victory. I don't know if a three-point tie is the right solution, but I know a shootout is the wrong one.

"If the Blackhawks season came down to a shootout and I could take any goalie in franchise history, it would be Tony Esposito. 'Tony O' is easily the franchise's most accomplished goaltender of all time.

"For my shooter I'd take Jonathan Toews. I'm not just picking 'Captain Serious' because he's the superstar of my generation, I'm picking him because he's a natural leader, he's ice cold under pressure, and generally hovers around a 50 percent success rate."

Colorado Avalanche

JULIE FELDER

"I am a relatively new fan of hockey. Over the past few years and as a Lake Erie Monsters fan, I would follow the boys' careers. As they were getting called up, I naturally became a fan of the Avs!

"While I wish that overtime were longer, I am a fan of the shootout. I think that it gives great excitement and closure to the game. I can't imagine playing an entire game and leaving with a tie.

"Definitely calling on Patrick Roy for the game-winning save!

"As for the shooter, I pick Matt Duchene. Matt is an exceptional young player that does well under pressure."

Columbus Blue Jackets

TIMOTHY GASSEN

"I've been a fan of the Blue Jackets since they came to life in 2000.

"I prefer the shootout because I believe a game as competitive as ice hockey deserves a definitive winner. The shootout preserves the excitement of a game's climax (rather than the stall tactics of a certain tie) and gives a heightened opportunity for fans to see the most skilled players at a critical moment.

"If the season came down to a shootout, my Blue Jackets goalie would be an obvious choice: 2013 Vezina winner Sergei Bobrovsky.

"For the shooter I'll go with a less obvious pick, R. J. Umberger. Admittedly, the pick is less for his offensive acumen than for his gritty and inspirational play over six seasons in my native Columbus."

Dallas Stars

Lisa Samuels

"I have been a Dallas Stars fan since they moved to Dallas in 1993 and I like the shootout. It brings out an opportunity to not only pick up an extra point but showcase your goalie and best players.

"If the Stars' season came down to a shootout and I could take any goalie in franchise history, hands down it would be Eddie (The Eagle) Belfour. The shooter would be none other than Mike Modano. Need I say more, number one United States–born player."

Detroit Red Wings

Jeff Januszek

"I have been a Red Wings fan for twenty-one years.

"I don't necessarily understand why there was uproar over the shootout being implemented into the NHL. There is nothing exciting about a tie. Ties suck.

"If I had to choose one Red Wings goaltender to be my shootout anchor, it would have to be Dominik Hasek. His personality matched his insane style of play, making him the perfect shootout goalie.

"As for my shooter pick, I'm going to go with a Russian . . . *not* the one you're thinking of though. I would pick Igor Larionov, the professor, as my go-to puck handler.

If Pavel Datsyuk is a Russian hockey God, Larionov is Zeus. Larionov is the perfect shootout pick."

Edmonton Oilers

DARCEY MCLAUGHLIN

"I can't quite remember when I became an Edmonton Oilers fan. It started with Gretzky, I know that.

"In a choice between a tie and the shootout, I take the shootout. Sports is about winning and losing. Not playing an entire contest to end up right back where you started. And a shootout does provide a lot of excitement, more so in person than on television. There is a real electricity in a building when it comes down to a shootout.

"As for whom I would have on the ice in a shootout on the last day with a playoff berth on the line, well, there's really no room for discussion when it comes to the Oilers. It has to be Grant Fuhr and Wayne Gretzky."

Florida Panthers

KEITH EVOLA

"I have been a Florida Panther fan for the last thirteen years.

"I am a big fan of the shootout. In a game, any game, there should be a winner and a loser. Ties are a big waste of time.

"If the season and a playoff position came down to a shootout, it would be a toss-up on the goalie. Roberto Luongo has been the best goalie for a franchise that has not been very good, but in that situation I would take John Vanbiesbrouck. Very good goalie who did very well in pressure situations.

"As far as the shooter . . . Pavel Bure. Best goal scorer that the Panthers ever had. If there was a player who you wanted to have the puck in a big spot . . . it was him."

Los Angeles Kings

JERRY HOUSER (PLAYED DAVE 'KILLER' CARLSON IN SLAP SHOT)

"I have been an LA Kings fan since the 1967-1968 season.

"I enjoy the shootout. Exciting and fun. The shootout offers a side of the game that is usually not seen during the game. The fact that both teams walk away with at least a point makes it worthwhile to have played the game and battled to a tie in regulation. I like that there is a final resolution to the game as opposed to simply end in a tie.

"Kings need a shootout win to make the playoffs and I have to pick a shooter and goalie for them. I have to go with Jonathan Quick. Over the years there have been some amazing shooters with incredible finesse. There are terrific shooters on the Kings today but to give a nod to the past I have to go with Ziggy Palffy."

Minnesota Wild

CARTER RODMAN

"I've been a fan of the Wild since I heard there was going to be an expansion team in Minnesota.

"I prefer the post-lockout system because it adds to the excitement of the game. Overtime often keeps me on the edge of my seat, but a shootout pushes me into this middle ground of terror and exhilaration.

"I'd have to go with Josh Harding as goalie. He isn't the best goalie we've ever had, but in a situation where it comes down to one moment, he's the guy I'd go with because he has the heart and determination of many men combined.

"As for my shooter, I'd have to go with Marian Gaborik. He was my favorite player growing up and the net seemed to be magnetic to the puck when it was on his stick. He had silky mitts and could dangle. I'd send him out for a sure goal."

Montreal Canadiens

Krista Eddy

"I've been a Montreal Canadiens fan for over ten years now.

"To be honest, as much as I find shootouts to be nerve-wracking, I much prefer them to the tie game where each team receives a point. In today's NHL, every single point counts, and I'd rather my team grabbing the two points instead of just one.

"Playoff spot on the line is a tough question. For my goaltender, I would have to pick Carey Price, as he is cool, calm, and collected in the net, and can very easily frustrate his opponents, making what seems like a difficult save an easy one. He's proven himself in high pressure situations (playoffs, World Juniors, and Olympics come to mind) and could no doubt handle the pressure of getting the win to hoist his team into the playoffs.

"As for my shooter, that's another tough one, but I'd have to pick Alex Galchenyuk. He has great hands and even better moves. He may be young, but he is only getting better with age, and would thrive upon the pressure of the situation that he found himself in."

Nashville Predators

Ray Harris

"I have been a Nashville Predators fan since April 2004.

"Ties aren't the worst thing ever, but I have to side with the post-lockout system of the shootout. I think it's a good way to break a draw even though it does come down to limited pockets of skill from either team.

"Last game of the season and we are in the shootout with a chance for the playoffs, and I have to pick a shooter. It would have to be Alex 'the defector' Radulov just nudging out Paul Kariya as my go-to guy. Radulov had phenomenal individual offensive talent. Breakaways and shootouts were his bread and butter.

"My go-to goalie—Chris Mason. I can't find the stats to back it up, but I remember him as a shootout beast."

New Jersey Devils

Matt Sweetwood

"I have been a Devils fan for twenty-five years.

"If I had to choose between the old system of ties and the new system of shootouts, I think the tie was a much better solution. The shootout really has very little to do with the actual game itself. As a Devils fan, if you look at last season, we had an absolutely horrific run of luck and lost thirteen shootouts (see "Devil of a Time") in a row and missed the playoffs as a result of that.

"If the Devils season came down to a shootout and I could take any goalie in franchise history in nets I'm going without question, no thought needed, I'm going with Marty Brodeur. He actually had such an amazing record in the shootout and he is a money player.

"For the shooter, that's a little more difficult, but I would probably say Ilya Kovalchuk. He also was money."

New York Islanders

LEITH BAREN

"I have been an Islander fan since day one and I prefer the possibility of a tie to the current system.

"If the Isles' season came down to a shootout, and I could take any goalie in franchise history, it would have to be Wade Dubielewicz. While no disrespect is meant to our greatest goaltender ever (Billy Smith), 'Dubie' was the winning goaltender in the biggest shootout our organization has ever won and therefore, he has earned another shot in a big moment.

"My shooter would be Frans Nielsen. At the current time, he has the best percentage of any NHL player in shootout history. I don't argue numbers."

New York Rangers

STEVE MURPHY

"I have been a Rangers Fan since the 1971-72 season.

"I always thought once it got to the shootout, I would be okay with the one point and it would feel the same as a tie did, but it doesn't. It still is a letdown but at the same time I like the excitement of knowing there is going to be a winner no matter what. In the end, I like the shootout, and I can honestly say I don't miss or long for a tie.

"If the Rangers' season came down to a shootout and I could take any goalie in franchise history in nets, it would be crazy to say anyone but Henrik Lundqvist. As far as the shooter, even though he wasn't in his prime when he was a Ranger, I would go with Eric Lindros in his prime."

Ottawa Senators

WILLIAM LOEWEN

"I have been a fan of the Ottawa Senators since they re-entered the league in the 1992-93 season.

"I was content with ties. If neither team has demonstrated that they deserve a win, why should they get one? I appreciate that the shootout adds excitement to the game, and I don't think it can be replaced with anything better.

"If I had to pick two current era players for a must-win shootout, I would probably go with Dominik Hasek in goal and, the Captain, Daniel Alfredsson in his prime as the shooter."

Philadelphia Flyers

SCOTT BORDEN

"I have been a Flyers fan since birth.

"Call me an anti-purist, but I actually prefer a shootout. While I acknowledge that some teams make or miss the playoffs based on a gimmick this way, when people spend $100+ to go see a game, they deserve to see a winner and a loser.

"If the Flyers' season came down to a shootout, which it did one time, and I could take any goalie in franchise history, I am going with a short tenured Flyer, but a goaltending legend. John Vanbiesbrouck would have been amazing in shootouts, so he gets the call!

"For my shooter, I'll take Claude Giroux who has every move in the book. I was tempted to go with (Daniel) Briere or (Eric) Lindros, but Claude makes excellent goalies look awfully silly with some of his shootout inventions."

Pittsburgh Penguins

BRIAN CUBAN

"I have been a Pittsburgh Penguin fan since I was first old enough to appreciate the game, probably when I was eleven years old.

"I prefer the post-lockout system of a shootout. I believe it makes the game more fun to watch.

"Last game of the season and the Penguins need the extra point in the shootout to make the playoffs, my choice for goalie would be Tom Barrasso. For the shooter, Mario, of course. Mario Lemieux is my era, my star, and he saved hockey in Pittsburgh."

San Jose Sharks

LARRY LEAVITT

"I have been following the Sharks since they started up in 1991-92 season, but became a die-hard fan when I moved back to the San Francisco bay area in 2002."

"I would like to see other options before going to the shootout. It takes the 'team sport' aspect out of the game.

"If the Sharks need a shootout win on the last day to make the playoffs, I would ultimately go with Calder Memorial Trophy winner Evgeni Nabokov. As for the shooter, there are so many to choose from but I would have to give the nod to the man who called the shot before he even took it in an all-star game . . . Owen Nolan."

St Louis Blues

GARY THOMAS

"Been a fan of the St. Louis Blues since 1968.

"For me, I like the pre-lockout system of ending a game. I just think if two teams do battle and the game ends in a tie, then it stands as a tie. As for who I would have on the ice in a shootout on the last day with a playoff berth on the line, my goalie would have to be Glenn Hall and the shooter would be Brett Hull."

Tampa Bay Lightning

Peter Berman

"I have been a fan of the Bolts since they arrived here in Tampa.

"I like the post-lockout system. I hate a tie and there should be a winner in every game. The shootout provides an opportunity for the team to get two points and win.

"If the Lightning season came down to a shootout, and I could take any goalie in franchise history, it would have to be Nikolai Khabibulin. Tough question on the shooter, but I'd have to go with Marty, I like my chances with the puck on Martin St. Louis's stick."

Toronto Maple Leafs

Christopher Bolton

"I have been a Leafs fan for forty-four years.

"I hate the shootout. I think the shootout is the worst thing to come to hockey, in fact I shut them off. If a game goes to a shootout I turn the game off and I am done.

"If the Leafs' season came down to a shootout and I could take any goalie in franchise history, I'm going with Johnny Bower even though I love Mike Palmateer. Bower was probably a little stronger, and for my shooter I'll put the puck on Mats Sundin."

Vancouver Canucks

SULLY OF THE GREEN MEN

"I have been a fan of the Vancouver Canucks since I was four, so it's twenty-four years now, although Gretzky was the one that got me into the game.

"For me the post-lockout system of going to the shootout is a far better system. As a fan, I couldn't stand leaving the rink after witnessing a tie. It was brutal!

"If the Canucks' season came down to a shootout and I had to pick a guy to take a shot, well, that's an easy one as far as shooters go. Jarkko Ruutu hands down gets my vote! The guy was 'Mr. Automatic' in the extra, extra frame.

"As for goalies, hmm . . . that's hard to answer. Basically in Vancouver, if our shooters aren't perfect, we lose."

Washington Capitals

LULU HICKEY

"I became a Washington Capitals fan when we moved here from Germany in 2002.

"The shootouts are a very exciting part of the game! I enjoy the excitement that a shootout brings. All across the nation you can find fans who oppose or who are for the shootout but no matter what, I believe it does get the fans up on their feet and all wound up, ready to shout or boo as soon as the puck is shot.

"If there is a playoff spot on the line for the Capitals, I would choose Semyon Varlamov as my goalie.

"As my shooter, I would select Matt Hendricks. The last year Matt was with the Caps, he was tagged 'The Paralyzer' because of his unbelievable (or believable) pump fake that would make the opposing goalie drop down so quick they didn't know what hit them, virtually paralyzing the goalie. Matt was a guaranteed point in the shootout which put him in the top 20 shooters that goalies did not want to face."

Winnipeg Jets

Scott Macumber

"I have been a Jets fan since their return to Winnipeg.

"The shootout is very exciting for a fan. It puts your player and the other team's goalie on a one-on-one penalty shot type situation and the extra point gives you something to play for.

"I think the shootout should stay in the game for the fans' sake. The fans pay to watch these games. It should be as exciting as possible.

"If the Jets' season came down to a shootout and I could take any goalie in franchise history in nets, hands down it's Joe Daley. He backed the Jets to three AVCO Cups and for my shooter it's Teemu Selanne. Best player in Jets history."

Appendix

Shootout Records

Team Shootout Records

Entering the 2014-2015 season

(Skaters: Goals-Shooting, Percentage, Game Deciding Goals)
(Goaltenders: Won-Lost, Shots Against, Goals Against, SV%)

Anaheim Mighty Ducks

SKATERS	GOALS	PCT	GDG	
Corey Perry	25	36%	10	
Ryan Getzlaf	21	34%	5	
Ryan Kesler	11	24%	4	

GOALIE	W-L	SA	GA	SV%
Jason LaBarbera	12-11	79	34	.570

Arizona Coyotes

SKATERS	GOALS	PCT	GDG	
Sam Gagner	17	32%	9	
Martin Erat	16	32%	12	
Mikkel Boedker	11	32.4%	4	

GOALIE	W-L	SA	GA	SV%
Mike Smith	21-27	158	59	.628

Boston Bruins

SKATERS	GOALS	PCT	GDG	
Patrice Bergeron	22	33%	8	
David Krejci	12	31%	6	
Loui Eriksson	10	28%	4	

GOALIE	W-L	SA	GA	SV%
Tuukka Rask	15-14	111	34	.694

Buffalo Sabres

SKATERS	GOALS	PCT	GDG	
Brian Gionta	20	37%	7	
Matt Moulson	13	48%	5	
Drew Stafford	13	33%	3	

GOALIE	W-L	SA	GA	SV%
Michel Neuvirth	8-7	51	17	.667

Calgary Flames

SKATERS	GOALS	PCT	GDG	
Jiri Hudler	16	33%	5	
Devin Setoguchi	11	44%	5	
Mason Raymond	9	27%	5	

GOALIE	W-L	SA	GA	SV%
Miikka Kiprusoff	23-37	185	73	.605

Carolina Hurricanes

SKATERS	GOALS	PCT	GDG	
Alexander Semin	15	32%	6	
Jeff Skinner	6	29%	3	
Nathan Gerbe	4	36%	3	

GOALIE	W-L	SA	GA	SV%
Cam Ward	11-25	107	41	.617

Chicago Black Hawks

SKATERS	GOALS	PCT	GDG	
Jonathan Toews	34	50%	10	
Patrick Kane	30	39%	14	
Brad Richards	29	37%	13	

GOALIE	W-L	SA	GA	SV%
Corey Crawford	20-18	129	38	.705

Colorado Avalanche

SKATERS	GOALS	PCT	GDG	
Daniel Briere	21	39%	8	
Alex Tanguay	19	37%	9	
Matt Duchene	10	36%	5	

GOALIE	W-L	SA	GA	SV%
Semyon Varlamov	18-11	94	23	.755

Columbus Blue Jackets

SKATERS	GOALS	PCT	GDG	
Nathan Horton	12	28%	4	
Jack Johnson	10	28%	2	
Mark Letestu	9	45%	3	

GOALIE	W-L	SA	GA	SV%
Sergei Bobrovsky	11-11	66	24	.636

Dallas Stars

SKATERS	GOALS	PCT	GDG	
Jason Spezza	22	39%	9	
Ales Hemsky	21	36%	9	
Tyler Seguin	15	44%	6	

GOALIE	W-L	SA	GA	SV%
Kari Lehtonen	36-23	207	57	.725

Detroit Red Wings

SKATERS	GOALS	PCT	GDG	
Pavel Datsyuk	35	44%	10	
Henrik Zetterberg	13	25%	4	
Stephen Weiss	9	23%	6	

GOALIE	W-L	SA	GA	SV%
Jimmy Howard	19-21	143	40	.720

Edmonton Oilers

SKATERS	GOALS	PCT	GDG	
Jordan Eberle	14	47%	2	
Matt Hendricks	9	50%	5	
David Perron	9	28%	1	

GOALIE	W-L	SA	GA	SV%
Viktor Fasth	6-3	30	12	.600

Florida Panthers

SKATERS	GOALS	PCT	GDG	
Brad Boyes	37	46%	12	
Jussi Jokinen	33	43%	12	
Alex Kovalev	19	40%	7	

GOALIE	W-L	SA	GA	SV%
Roberto Luongo	34-41	265	87	.672

Los Angeles Kings

SKATERS	GOALS	PCT	GDG	
Anze Kopitar	30	40%	13	
Dustin Brown	19	33%	7	
Mike Richards	17	29%	6	

GOALIE	W-L	SA	GA	SV%
Jonathan Quick	36-22	206	61	.704

Minnesota Wild

SKATERS	GOALS	PCT	GDG	
Zach Parise	37	45%	10	
Mikko Koivu	36	43%	15	
Thomas Vanek	22	36%	6	

GOALIE	W-L	SA	GA	SV%
Niklas Backstrom	22-33	182	80	.560

Montreal Canadiens

SKATERS	GOALS	PCT	GDG	
David Desharnais	13	52%	6	
Pierre-Alexander Parenteau	11	46%	4	
Rene Bourque	8	31%	3	

GOALIE	W L	SA	GA	SV%
Carey Price	21-24	156	47	.699

Nashville Predators

SKATERS	GOALS	PCT	GDG	
Matt Cullen	23	41%	9	
Mike Ribeiro	22	35%	7	
Olli Jokinen	21	36%	9	

GOALIE	W-L	SA	GA	SV%
Pekka Rinne	23-23	175	51	.709

New Jersey Devils

SKATERS	GOALS	PCT	GDG	
Ilya Kovalchuk	24	39%	11	
Patrik Elias	22	34%	9	
Ryan Clowe	16	35%	11	

GOALIE	W-L	SA	GA	SV%
Scott Clemmensen	11-15	95	36	.621
**Martin Brodeur				

New York Islanders

SKATERS	GOALS	PCT	GDG	
Frans Nielsen	33	55%	15	
John Taveras	9	27%	2	
Mikhail Grabovski	8	31%	3	

GOALIE	W-L	SA	GA	SV%
Jaroslav Halak	19-20	129	40	.690

New York Rangers

SKATERS	GOALS	PCT	GDG	
Rick Nash	29	37%	11	
Lee Stempniak	12	32%	5	
Dan Boyle	10	28%	2	

GOALIE	W-L	SA	GA	SV%
Henrik Lundqvist	48-33	310	76	.755

Ottawa Senators

SKATERS	GOALS	PCT	GDG	
David Legwand	10	31%	4	
Kyle Turris	9	39%	3	
Milan Michalek	7	26%	1	

GOALIE	W-L	SA	GA	SV%
Craig Anderson	20-17	129	44	.659

Philadelphia Flyers

SKATERS	GOALS	PCT	GDG
Claude Giroux	17	43%	5
Vincent Lecavalier	14	25%	6
Matt Read	6	40%	1

GOALIE	W-L	SA	GA	SV%
Steve Mason	15-24	132	46	.652

Pittsburgh Penguins

SKATERS	GOALS	PCT	GDG
Sidney Crosby	26	42%	15
Evgeni Malkin	19	40%	8
Kris Letang	16	33%	9

GOALIE	W-L	SA	GA	SV%
Marc-Andre Fleury	45-19	205	47	.771

San Jose Sharks

SKATERS	GOALS	PCT	GDG
Joe Pavelski	29	39%	10
Logan Couture	14	42%	7
Patrick Marleau	14	34%	7

GOALIE	W-L	SA	GA	SV%
Antti Niemi	32-21	179	47	.737

St. Louis Blues

SKATERS	GOALS	PCT	GDG
T. J. Oshie	27	56%	14
Alexander Steen	14	45%	1
Peter Mueller	13	42%	5

GOALIE	W-L	SA	GA	SV%
Brian Elliott	15-16	108	38	.648

Tampa Bay Lightning

SKATERS	GOALS	PCT	GDG
Steven Stamkos	7	23%	3
Ryan Callahan	6	26%	4
Valterri Filppula	6	26%	3

GOALIE	W-L	SA	GA	SV%
Evgeni Nabokov	30-30	214	76	.645

Toronto Maple Leafs

SKATERS	GOALS	PCT	GDG
Phil Kessel	15	27%	13
Mike Santorelli	12	43%	5
Joffrey Lupul	11	44%	6

GOALIE	W-L	SA	GA	SV%
James Reimer	7	54	18	.667

Vancouver Canucks

SKATERS	GOALS	PCT	GDG
Radim Vrbata	35	43%	11
Alexandre Burrows	12	38%	2
Nick Bonino	6	46%	1

GOALIE	W-L	SA	GA	SV%
Ryan Miller	50-30	279	81	.710

Washington Capitals

SKATERS	GOALS	PCT	GDG
Alex Ovechkin	25	30%	8
Nicklas Backstrom	16	37%	6
Brooks Laich	6	33%	2

GOALIE	W-L	SA	GA	SV%
Braden Holtby	10-4	48	15	.688

Winnipeg Jets

SKATERS	GOALS	PCT	GDG
Blake Wheeler	16	38%	2
Andrew Ladd	13	45%	7
Bryan Little	12	32%	5

GOALIE	W-L	SA	GA	SV%
Ondrej Pavelec	15-19	119	43	.639

Contributors

We want to thank all those associated with the sport of hockey and those who were not directly involved, but were passionate about the game nonetheless, who made this book possible

Kenny Albert is the radio play-by-play voice of the New York Rangers and works as a TV play-by-play broadcaster for the NHL on NBC.

Gary Bettman is the commissioner of the National Hockey League.

Larry Brooks is one of the foremost authorities on the sport of hockey. *The Hockey News* listed Brooks among the "Top 100 People of Power and Influence in the NHL" a record seven times.

Craig Button is a former general manager of the Calgary Flames.

Bill Clement is a former two-time Stanley Cup Champion and co-host of NHL Live.

Jim Devellano is the Senior Vice-President and Alternate Governor of the Detroit Red Wings.

Mike "Doc" Emrick is the lead play-by-play announcer for national telecasts of NHL games on NBC Sports and NBC Sports Network.

Emrick was the recipient of the 2008 Foster Hewitt Memorial Award for outstanding contributions to hockey broadcasting. In 2011, he became the first member of the media to be inducted into the United States Hockey Hall of Fame.

Phil Esposito is a Hall of Famer, and a former head coach and general manager in the NHL.

Mike Eruzione was the Captain of the 1980 United States Olympic Hockey team that upset the Soviet Union and won the Gold Medal.

Stan Fischler (a.k.a. "The Hockey Maven") has covered hockey for over fifty years and has written over ninety books on the sport. Fischler is widely considered the top historian of the sport.

Angelo "Zig" Fracassi is a sports talk show host on Sirius XM Satellite Radio and a contributor to "NHL Home Ice."

Kerry Fraser is a former senior referee in the National Hockey League who has officiated over 1300 regular season games and thirteen Stanley Cup Finals.

Matt Harvey is a pitcher for the New York Mets.

Dave Hanson is a former NHL defenseman who was cast as one of the Hanson brothers in the hockey movie classic *Slap Shot*.

Pat Hickey has been a hockey columnist for the *Montreal Gazette* for the past ten years.

Mark Howe is a former NHL defenseman, a member of the World Hockey Association Hall of Fame and the son of Hall of Famer and all-time great, Gordie Howe.

E. J. Hradek is a regular co-host for *NHL Live* on NHL Network. Hradek spent thirteen years as Senior Writer for *ESPN The Magazine* and was part of the original staff that helped launch the publication in 1998. Hradek is a regular contributor to *Hockey Night Live* on MSG-TV.

Billy Jaffe is a former hockey player for the University of Michigan and has been a hockey broadcaster for NHL games since the 1998-99 season.

Mike Keenan is a former head coach in the National Hockey League who was behind the bench for the 1993-94 Stanley Cup–winning New York Rangers.

Mick Kern is an on-air host for Sirius XM NHL Radio.

Don LaGreca is the co-host of *The Michael Kay Show* on ESPN-NY, 98.7 in New York and is a play-by-play voice for the New York Rangers.

Lou Lamoriello is the New Jersey Devils' president, CEO and general manager. His interview is courtesy of Sirius XM NHL Network's *Hockey This Morning* with Mike Ross and Mick Kern.

Craig Ludwig is a former defenseman who was the alternate Captain on the Dallas Stars Stanley Cup–winning team in 1999.

Pierre LeBrun is a hockey insider for the *Vancouver Sun*. LeBrun has worked on *Hockey Night in Canada* telecasts and writes a column for ESPN.com.

Bill Lekas is a sports talk show host and update anchor on Sirius XM Satellite Radio.

Steve Levy has been with ESPN since 1993 as a *SportsCenter* anchor and NHL broadcaster.

Doug MacLean is a former NHL head coach and general manager.

Dave Maloney is a former defenseman for the New York Rangers and is the color analyst on radio broadcasts.

Paul Maurice is the head coach of the Winnipeg Jets.

"Jiggs" McDonald has broadcast NHL games for more than forty years.

Pierre McGuire is best known for being the analyst on "Inside the Glass" during NBC Sports telecasts of National Hockey League games.

Bob McKenzie has covered hockey for TSN since 1986. McKenzie was a columnist for *The Toronto Star* for six years and was the editor-in-chief for *The Hockey News* for nine years.

Terry Mercury is a host on Sirius XM Radio's *Ice Cap*.

Mark Messier is a Hall of Famer, two-time Hart Trophy winner, Conn Smythe winner and six-time Stanley Cup champion.

Joe Micheletti is a former NHL defenseman and color analyst on New York Rangers broadcasts on MSG-TV.

Mike Milbury is a former NHL player, coach and executive who works as an analyst on NHL on NBC telecasts.

Craig Minervini is the radio voice of the Florida Panthers.

Bryan Murray is the general manager of the Ottawa Senators and has compiled over 600 victories as a head coach.

Ed Olczyk played 16 seasons in the NHL and was a member of the Stanley Cup-winning New York Rangers in 1994. Olczyk is the lead analyst, working with "Doc" Emrick, for the NHL on NBC and the NHL on NBC Sports Network.

Deb Placey is a co-host of *NHL Live* and has been with the MSG Network covering hockey since the mid-1990s.

Howie Rose is the TV play-by-play voice of the New York Islanders and was formerly the radio voice of the New York Rangers.

Sam Rosen has been the TV voice of the New York Rangers since the 1986-87 season.

Glen Sather is the president and general manager of the New York Rangers.

Peter Schwartz is an update anchor on CBS Sports Radio.

Neil Smith is a former general manager of the New York Rangers and New York Islanders.

Steve Somers is a radio sports talk show host who has been with WFAN radio in New York since their inception in 1987.

Pete Weber has been the voice of the Nashville Predators since their inception in the 1998-99 season.

Scott Wetzel is a sports talk show host on Sirius XM Mad Dog Radio.

Players (Current and Former in Alphabetical Order)

Nicklas Backstrom	Clint Malarchuk
Josh Bailey	Stephane Matteau
Martin Biron	Dominic Moore
Bryan Berard	Jayson More
Patrice Bergeron	Ken Morrow
Sergei Bobrovsky	Rick Nash
Henry Boucha	Michal Neuvirth
Brian Boucher	Bernie Nicholls
Dan Boyle	Frans Nielsen
Casey Cizikas	P. A. Parenteau
Logan Couture	Brad Park
Rick DiPietro	Tuukka Rask
Jhonas Enroth	Mark Scheifele
Loui Eriksson	Darryl Sittler
Nick Fotiu	Marc Staal
Nathan Gerbe	Drew Stafford
Adam Graves	Derek Stepan
Ron Greschner	Malcolm Subban
Glenn Healy	Cam Talbot
Anders Hedberg	Stephen Valiquette
Corey Hirsch	Gilles Villemure
Cory Hodgson	Jakub Voracek
Brent Johnson	Cam Ward
Derek King	Joel Ward
David Krejci	Kevin Weekes
Henrik Lundqvist	Jason Woolley
Kevin Kaminski	John Tavares
Nick Kypreos	Mike Veisor
Brooks Laich	Kurt Walker
Mark Letestu	Mats Zuccarello

Acknowledgments

Over the last six years of doing *SportstalkNy*, I have read hundreds of books. Like many others, I do not always take the time to read the Acknowledgments. Having gone through the process of writing a book, I now know how important these pages are to those preceding them, since without the names I am about to list, there would have been no *Shoot to Thrill*.

I would like to thank the following members of the press who welcomed me into their workplaces with open arms and showed me the ropes, including Ken Albert, Christian Arnold, Larry Brooks, Matt Calamia, Rick "Carpy" Carpinello, Jim Cerny, Scott Charles, Russ Cohen, Charles Curtis, Brett Cyrgalis, Bob Gelb, John Giannone, Denis Gorman, Andrew Gross, Sean Hartnett, Patrick Kearns, Allan Kreda, Brad Kurtzberg, Pat Leonard, Brian Monzo, Ira Podell, Seth Rothman, Arthur Staple, Katie Strang, Chayim Tauber, and Steve Zipay.

Thank you to Frank Brown and the NHL offices for setting up an interview with the commissioner, since no book on the shootout would have been complete without his voice. Thank you, too, to the New York Rangers PR department, John Rosasco, Ryan Nissan, Lindsay Ganghamer, and Michael Rappaport; the PR department of the New York Islanders, Kimber Auerbach and Jesse Eisenberg; the Boston Bruins PR department, Eric Tosi; the Washington Capitals PR Department, Sergey Kocharov and Megan Eichenberg; the Buffalo Sabres PR department Chris Dierken; the San Jose Sharks Media Relations Staff; the Columbus Blue Jackets PR department, Glenn Odebralski; and the Montreal Canadiens PR department.

Thanks also to the hundreds of authors who have appeared on *WLIE 540am SportstalkNy* for inspiring me over the years. I'm grateful as well to our loyal sponsors Leith Baren, Neil Cohen, Gary Pincus, Robert Solomon, and David and Andrew Reale, as well as my co-host AJ Carter, since without them none of this would have been possible.

The staff at Sports Publishing—in particular, Niels Aaboe (who gave a rookie a shot)—deserves thanks as well.

Last but not least my writing partner in this project, Howie Karpin, as he was the Phil Esposito to my Ken Hodge. Our method of collaborating was simple: I would do an interview, send him the audio tapes, and he would bury it in the back of the net!

—Mark Rosenman

When acknowledging those who supported me in the creation of this book, I have to start with my beautiful wife, Kathy, who has been with me all the way for over thirty-five years. I'm so proud of my two sons, Danny and Jake, and my "furry" son, Rex Karpin. My sister Carol and her husband, Barry Shore have always been behind me throughout the years. Thanks also to my nieces, Wendy and Sharon, and their children.

Thanks, too, to my supportive friends: Jay Brustman, Colm and Sascha Cahill, Rich Coutinho, Anthony DiGiovanni, Richard Fedderman, Mark Feinman, Corey Friedman, Rick Goldfarb, Mike Mancuso, Mike Mascaling, Tommy Matthews, Jay Nadler, Stu and Barbara Oppenheimer, Joe Pinto, Lew Rose, and Gary Simon.

—Howie Karpin